Why I Became a Professional Genealogist

A Case Study

LaWanna Lease Blount, PhD

iUniverse, Inc.
New York   Bloomington

iUniverse books may be ordered through booksellers or by contacting:

iUniverse
1663 Liberty Drive
Bloomington, IN 47403
www.iuniverse.com
1-800-Authors (1-800-288-4677)

ISBN: 978-1-4401-7821-4 (pbk)
ISBN: 978-1-4401-7822-1 (ebk)

Printed in the United States of America

iUniverse rev. date: 4/5/2010

Table of Contents

Why Study Genealogy And Become A Professional Genealogist? 1

Introduction 1

Review Of The Literature 3

The Historical Leadership Road Of Professional Genealogy 10

Research Methodology 19

Years Involved In Genealogy 23

Why I Became Interested In Genealogy 25

Why I Began To Study Genealogy 34

Why I Became A Professional Genealogist 48

Years As A Professional Genealogist And Education 59

Professional Tasks Carried Out And Time Spent As
  Professional Genealogists. 66

Conclusions And Model Of Why I Became A Professional Genealogist . . 74

Recommendations For Further Research 77

Endnotes 79

References 85

Appendices. 91

Tables with percentages for Table 8 92

Questionnaire. 94

Acknowledgements:

First, I thank all of my respondents to my questionnaire for their thoughtful responses, which made this study so interesting.

Thank you to: Lynn C. McMillion, Executive Director of the BCG for information on categories and numbers of BCG certifications.

A special thank you to the following people who assisted me in this research project by reviewing the manuscript and the questionnaire, and/or by answering my questions: Donn Devine, J.D., Dr. Carl Lindgren, Ms Peggy Baldwin, Dr. Carolyn Ybarra, Dr. Ruth Huffman-Hine, and Dr. David McDonald.

Why Study Genealogy And Become A Professional Genealogist?

Introduction

The last two decades have seen a dramatic rise in interest in genealogical study. The numbers have greatly increased since Internet tools have become so accessible and more are being added each day. No current studies tell us how many persons are involved in studying genealogy. Among the more serious genealogists, interest in becoming a professional genealogist is increasing. Today, over 1,800 self-described professional genealogists belong to a professional genealogists' group, with one hundred joining this group each year.[1]

Over the past two decades, journalists have written extensively about the increasing interest in "roots mania"[2]and why this frenzied interest has become so strong. Many have attributed it to Alex Haley's *Roots,* [3] as well as increased access to the Internet and to the resources available there. However, no studies have asked people why they seriously study genealogy and why serious genealogists have decided to become professionals. For some time now, this researcher has seen the need for exploratory research to shed some light on these questions. Has this avalanche of interest resulted from the increase in resources available via computers? Is it the result of an increased mobility of families moving through the country because of their careers, leaving kinfolk behind? Or has it been the consequence of a rapidly developing "fatherless society"?[4] This author wanted to determine the main reason for the respondents' serious pursuit of genealogical research, including many professionals who are pursuing the field's rigorous processes of credentialing. In addition, who is continuously pursuing formal continuing education/ seminars and national conferences, and why?

Purpose of the Study

The purpose of this exploratory case study was twofold:

1. to determine the main reason why professional genealogists began to study genealogy
2. to determine why these individuals decided to become professionals

Professionalism

In *Professional Genealogy*,[5] the major textbook for professional genealogists and for courses in genealogical degree programs, Devine states,

> For success, the professional genealogist is expected to exhibit the characteristics of any profession. In sum: a mastery of a body of knowledge, expertise in applying it, a reasonable degree of business acumen, a commitment to intellectual growth, conformity to accepted conventions, observance of peer enforced standards of work and conduct, membership in professional organizations and pursuit of the professional credentials that represent the field.[6]

Devine reminds us that in practice, our expertise is reflected in the quality of our work over time. However, the public looks at surrogate measures and finds them in four areas:

1. *Certification or licensing*–to assure consumers that their practitioners perform at a minimum level of competence within published ethical codes.
2. *Service in the public interest*–often on a pro-bono basis, which originated in the medieval professions of arms, law, medicine, and religion.
3. *Conformity to basic conventions*–in effect, conformity to the widely recognized and accepted ways of doing things.
4. *Comparison to other learned professions*–in dress, ethics, manners and speech (Often the initial bases on which professionalism is judged).[7]

Review Of The Literature

In my comprehensive review of the literature, I searched mass magazines, newspapers, and journals of general interest, in addition to peer-reviewed academic journals. I was interested in reading material to learn what the public had been reading about genealogy during the last three decades, related to the oft-noted surging interest in genealogy, and to seek any research studies that had focused on the interest in genealogy during that time.

Historical Perspectives of Interest in Genealogy

It is important to view the fluctuations in the growth of genealogical interest during the last two decades from the perspective of the historical events propelling the trend, along with the historical growth of the professionalization of genealogical studies.

The *Stebbins Genealogy*, published in 1771, was the first American-published genealogy However, not surprisingly, there was little cultural appetite for genealogical pursuits. Americans were excited about building a utopia of equality, and tracing hereditary lines emitted social distinction that was regarded with disdain.[8] During the 1840s, genealogy began to gather a bit of strength. The New England Historic Genealogical Society (NEHGS) was established in 1845 with the purpose of collecting, preserving, and occasionally publishing genealogical matter related to early New England families.[9] In 1847, the NEHGS inaugurated the *New England Historical and Genealogical Register*, the first quarterly that was devoted entirely to genealogical studies. According to Taylor and Crandall, during the succeeding decade, 96 primary genealogies appeared in the *Register*.[10]

Can we assume then that once America became a nation with historical significance, the early families who had founded the nation were interested in leaving a legacy for their descendants, although they may have, in an earlier period, looked with disdain at families attesting to social distinctions?

After the Civil War and World War I, there was an avalanche of genealogical materials and books, and increased readership. The national centennial celebrations in 1876 gave rise to numerous local and regional histories, featuring brief family sketches of leading members of local communities. Family reunions began to develop, as did patriotic and hereditary associations or lineage societies, such as the Sons of the American Revolution and Colonial Dames, especially after 1890. The National Genealogical Society (NGS) was established in 1903, fostering a scholarly approach to genealogical research. Ultimately, what came to be known as the Jacobus School of scholarly genealogy was launched[11] in 1922, with the publication of Jacobus's journal, ultimately known as *The American Genealogist*, which was and remains (arguably) the genealogy field's premier independent scholarly voice.

The vast changes during the reconstruction years, and the beginning of industry and mass production with its overcrowded cities wrought mainly by the influx of immigrants, resulted in problems of sanitation, health, fire, and transportation.[12] Especially critical and lasting were the economic changes affecting the family. The production of goods created new kinds of jobs, and young men could choose new occupations, different from those of their fathers. With the creation of factories and mills, young women also worked and could choose lifestyles that were unlike those of their mothers.

The movement of men's work outside the home in the mid-1800s created "separate spheres for men and women." The man's sphere was the paid-work world outside the home, while the women were to take care of the home and the children--a change from the family productive enterprise. This was the beginning of the age of individualization.[13]

The family unit was threatened by the industrialization of society and the rapidly increasing influx of immigrants, which some people believed threatened the solidarity of the current Anglo-Saxon culture of America.[14] According to Cherlin, the scale of immigration from 1850 to World War I was massive. In 1850, 10 percent of the population had been born in another country; by 1880, this figure had increased to 13 percent; and by 1910 it was 15 percent.[15]

During these years of change and fear for the family unit, people increasingly sought their kinsmen for moral and family guidance. These troubled times resulted in a great increase in interest in genealogy, family reunions, and associations.[16] "With misgivings about the individual's place in a complex world, about the solidarity of the family unit, and about the locus of power in a pluralistic society, individuals reached out to living kin for assistance and reclaimed appropriate ancestors for guideposts."[17]

Genealogy finalized its first major phase of development in the late 19th and early 20th centuries. The first International Congress of Genealogy met in San Francisco in July of 1915.[18]

By the 1980s, according to Taylor and Crandall, a half million Americans and Canadians were generally considered active genealogists. One thousand genealogical societies existed in America and Canada, and 300, 000 Americans were members of genealogical societies.[19]

Since that time, there has been a great deal of concern about the family. Fatherless homes, single-sex marriages, child abuse, same-sex adoption of children, increasing divorce, surrogacy, the increase in step-families, and social policies related to adoption and birth technologies are all catalysts for societal debate. Concomitant fear fosters an increasing interest in genealogy. Again, families appear to turn to their kinsmen for guidance and advice in challenging phases.

No studies have addressed why people began to study genealogy and why they became professionals; however, Alex Haley's book *Roots* and its televised miniseries seemed to arouse an explosion of interest in genealogical study over the past two decades.

The Genealogy Tidal Wave of the 1990s

An unprecedented surge began in the 1990s, with the advent of the Internet and the development of new technologies. In addition, the increasing interest brought about by journalists in their writings in the mass magazines and newspapers fueled "family tree climbers" with renewed energy in their hunt for ancestors.

"A fascination with ancestry has long been part of the human condition, from the 'begats' of the Bible to the *Roots* miniseries and the restoration of Ellis Island. But with the advent of the Internet and new technology, genealogy has entered a new age."[20] Seabrook, writing of the new DNA testing, remarked, "Our Founding Fathers abolished the hereditary aristocracy, but in its place we have an extraordinary variety of hereditary societies; early-settler societies, religious societies, and ethnic societies."[121] In addition, the seductive, compelling stories of people and what "Jenni Genes" found on the Internet and in the resources in libraries and their exclamations of the "joy of the hunt" stimulated others to join the fun and start to climb their family tree. Clearly, "the biggest boon to the heritage hunt has been cyberspace. No one has been more influential there than Cyndi Howells, a housewife of Puyallup, Washington, who became obsessed with genealogy after tracing her own family tree."[22] Howells quit her job at a bank and began her website of genealogical links in 1996. She started with 1,000 links in March of that year, and by November 1996, her website offered more than 9,600 links in more than 50 categories. It was featured in *Newsweek* on February 24, 1997; *on NBC Nightly News with Tom Brokaw* in May 1999; in the *Wall Street Journal* in 2001; and in *USA Today* in October 2002. Cyndi's list currently has more than 251,235 links. She has an average of 2 million page hits each month.[23]

News articles continued to illustrate this frenzy. For example, a 1997 *Alberta Report* story quoted Vonn McDonald, owner of a tour company in Calgary and herself an amateur genealogist: "It showed you could do it yourself. You don't need to go to some expensive researcher to find your family history."[24]

"Spurred by new resources on the Internet, the ranks of amateur genealogists are growing, and millions of family trees are flourishing."[25] Krum noted, "Digging through attics, old photo albums, and libraries, more than l.5 million Americans are getting to their roots via the Web." "The Net has opened many research windows," Krum quoted Shirley Langdon Wilcox, then -president of the NGS. "While families have become more complex, people are still interested in finding out where they came from."[26] During the last decade, increased technology has spawned many software programs, helping the work in genealogy to become more professional. Kindaris ranks these software programs into categories, based on their functionality to assist users in selecting the best program for them.[34]

The new Ellis Island website—a database for searching for ancestors who immigrated to the United States—was proclaimed more popular in its first week than Britney Spears, Pokemon, and *Survivor*."

The site attracted so much interest that an estimated 85 percent of users were turned away from www.ellisislandrecords.org during the first few days after its launch. In the site's first six hours, it recorded eight million hits and currently attracts 25 million to 27 million hits a day.[27]

The *Seattle Times* focused on the age of people chasing their roots: "The new face of genealogy is represented by people in their 30s, 40s, and 50s." "More than ever, baby boomers—who spent their youths militantly uninterested in anything as bourgeois as family history—are tracing their roots. And they're going at it with a vengeance." "For boomers swept cross-country by careers and now isolated from kith and kin, genealogy offers a way back home." "Others seek to reclaim the ethnic heritage that their immigrant ancestors labored so mightily to shed. Some are adoptees searching for birth parents. All seem to enjoy the detective work, the addictive tow of the search, the 'aha!' of discovery. But at its essence, genealogy offers yet another way for boomers to focus on their favorite topic: Themselves...."[28]

Maritz Study

Maritz Marketing Research found that four in ten adults (or 113 million) are at least somewhat interested in genealogy.[29]Adults aged 65 and older and those aged 18 to 24 are less likely than others to be at least somewhat involved in genealogy, at 39 percent for each group. This study revealed that the highest rates of genealogical interest were among middle-aged people. Half of adults aged 45 to 64 are at least somewhat involved in genealogy, as are 47 percent of those aged 35 to 44, and 46 percent of 25-to-34-year olds. However, enthusiasm for the hobby is strongest among adults aged 35 to 44. Nine percent say they are involved a great deal in genealogy. This group is the most likely of all adults to be married and have young children. It was suggested that their interest in genealogy may be driven by a sense of rootlessness at home and in life in dual-earner households.

Ancestry Study

In December 2007, Ancestry.com conducted a survey to determine how much people knew about their roots.[30] This survey was commissioned by The Generations Network, the parent company of Ancestry.com. While the bias and the resulting lack of validity in this survey are apparent, it is not surprising that the results indicated that young Americans were interested in their roots. Eighty-three percent of 18- to 34-year-olds expressed an interest in learning their family history. Following closely behind were the 35- to 54-year olds at 77 percent and Americans aged 55 and older at 73 percent.

The study also indicated that half of Americans knew the name of only one or none of their great-grandparents. Twenty-two percent of Americans did not know what either of their grandfathers did or had done for a living. While 78 percent of Americans said they were interested in learning more about their family history, fifty percent of American families had never researched their roots.

Bishop focused on learning why individuals conducted genealogical research.[31] His question was "Do individuals who conduct genealogical research see their work as compiling a collection—a collection of relatives?" His article was an attempt to combine his continuing exploration of collecting behavior with the interest in learning more about why individuals conduct genealogical research. He maintains that baby boomers, many of them motivated by the desire to learn or to confirm the history of their collections, have fueled this surge. Bishop contends that currently popular television shows such as *Antiques Roadshow* and A&E's *The Incurable Collector* are only the most visible representations of our fascination with collecting, and that there are deeper reasons that we are becoming our collections. He cites Jean Baudrillard who believes that we collect to reconnect with the past, with nature, and with divinity, as collectibles represent "absolute reality."[32]

Bishop did not attest to any knowledge that he had about the training of professional genealogists, their certification, continuing education studies, enrollment in degree courses, or what they do as professionals. However, he did address the role of professionals from a critical stance that illustrated a lack of knowledge about professional genealogists and what they do. Bishop suggested that journalists provide the stage for skilled genealogists to tell their stories and to develop a demand for the services offered by genealogists who have mastered what they have "deemed the necessary skills."[33] This would be an attempt <u>by professional genealogists,</u> playing the role of "cultural cartography." Hobbyists are reminded of their status as apprentices. They must partake of the instruction offered by professionals before they can be officially admitted "to the profession." The increasing interest in genealogy makes it more newsworthy; as a result, journalists cover genealogy more often.

Professional Genealogists' Image

While it is true that news writers and journalists have the eyes and ears of the mass of people who are fascinated with their "tree climbing" stories, professional genealogists must step forward and clarify the skills and standards of genealogical research. Quite possibly, the writing of more articles about what genealogists actually do would help the professional genealogist's image.

<u>Respondents of this study</u>

In the present study, 48.2 percent of the 83 genealogist respondents delivered presentations at seminars and conferences; 49.4 percent taught genealogy courses; 48.2 percent wrote about genealogy; and 79.5 percent did contract work for clients.

DNA Literature

Recent work in DNA analysis has stirred up another new area of interest and another way of finding our ancestors. A news story captured the interest of the would-be hobby genealogist: "They don't want your blood, just your spit. Geri Gibbons, of Madison, nabbed her 65–year-old uncle during his first trip to the U.S. from Scotland in September. Armed with a cotton swab, she swiped a swath of DNA-laden tissue from his mouth. 'I'm not entirely sure he knew what I was asking for,' she says, 'but he didn't seem to mind.'"[35] A 1998 *Forbes* Magazine asked, "What's Blond and Blue-Eyed and read all over? Icelandic DNA. It is going to figure in the hundreds of millions of dollars a year that drug companies are pouring into genetic research. Why? Because Icelanders, 270,000 of them, have the clearest bloodlines on the planet and now drug companies want to trace those lines to genes underlying disease and it will cost."[36]

John Seabrook stated, "DNA is a vast new archive of human history, one that can be used both for answering questions about one's own ancestors and for shedding light on the ancestry of the human species."[37]

While the literature reviewed does not specifically address the role of the professional genealogist, the genealogical literature does attend to this area.

The Historical Leadership Road Of Professional Genealogy

In the analyses of the questionnaire responses, I turned back to the data that exists in the literature on the scholarly and leadership role of genealogy throughout its history. Three undergirding elements can be identified as reasons for the rapid growth of professionals in the genealogy field, as evidenced in the literature and the responses of the respondents to the questionnaire of the present study. They are:

1. Continual leadership at the national level
2. Support of education and continuing education
3. Continuing development and enforcement of high standards of the profession

The Interaction of Leadership, Education, and Standards of the Profession Toward a Theory of the Developing Professional Genealogist

Throughout its history, the field of genealogical study has been marked with outstanding leadership in its organizational configurations, its procedures, its support of the scholarly development of professionals, and its building and enforcement of standards of the profession.

Jacobus School

The Jacobus School was launched in the 1930s for the purpose of developing a scholarly approach to genealogy with elected fellows (currently limited to fifty) committed to a scholarly approach to genealogical research, as well as instilling professionalism. Since that time, exemplary leadership has focused on improving and updating genealogy, in an effort to stay up with the trends of the current times. Indeed, the current leadership model is in concert with the well-known leadership model for this information society and what is known as "leadership of the learning organization."[38]

This model of professional leadership spans organizations, multimodal systems, and international groups. This leadership is strong, as indicated by the achievements and responses of the respondents of this research study. The implementation of leadership here may well be the prototype model of the "learning society of the 21st century." However, more research is needed to integrate and to clarify the various components of this leadership model.

Mills identifies four "standard-bearers" in the field of genealogy that were the result of the Jacobus School of scholarly genealogy:[39]

1. In 1940, the American Society of Genealogists was composed of fifty elected fellows who were scholars in the field of genealogy and were committed to upgrade standards in genealogical development.
2. In 1950, the National Institute for Genealogical Research (NIGR) was launched at the National Archives.
3. In 1964, Samford University's Institute of Genealogy and Historical Research (IGHR) began a premier week-long residential program taught by the top scholars in the field.
4. In 1964, the Board for Certification of Genealogists (BCG), an independent agency, was born.

These standard-bearers are indeed shaping the professionalism of the field of genealogy through their strong and effective leadership, not only in policy-making, but also in the implementation of those policies and programs along with their scholarly publications. Their leaders' work reflects a growing interest in professionalism in genealogy.

NGS

The development of the professional genealogist sprouted with the organization and development of the National Genealogical Society (NGS) in 1903. Education was one of NGS's primary goals; thus, lectures, conferences, courses, programs, and publications were designed as instructional material. With the sponsorship of lectures, audio teleconferences, and, later, on-line lectures, NGS educated the genealogical community in scholarly genealogy. In 1981, with its *American Genealogy: A Basic Course*, NGS came to be regarded as a leader in the field of genealogical education.[40]

In 1978, NGS sponsored the Diamond Jubilee Conference in Silver Spring, Maryland. In 1981, it began its annual Conference in the States—a series of educational conferences that allowed people to learn, share, interact, and share ideas.[41] These national conferences, with 200 to 250 presenters, have drawn 1,600 to 2,000 persons from various parts of the United States.[42]

During these conferences, NGS sponsors seminars known as skillbuilders, which further develop standards among the participants. NGS also publishes the *National Genealogical Society Quarterly*, which was established in 1912 and evolved into a recognized scholarly, peer-reviewed publication. NGS also publishes the *NGS Magazine: Guidelines on Standards,* as well as sponsors research trips, and bestows annual awards to scholars in the field.[43]

Conference Attendance by Respondents

The data in this study reveal that 29 (33.2 percent) of the 87 respondents had attended three to five national conferences over the past five years; an additional 25 (28.7 percent) of the respondents had attended one to two conferences during that same time period (see Table 15). A total of 54 of the 87 respondents (62 percent), then, had participated in at least one national conference within the past half-decade.

NGS Home Study Course Participation by Respondents

The NGS Home Study Course was second in popularity with the respondents: 28—nearly one-third of them --had participated in this course (Table 8).

IGHR

In 1962, the Institute for Genealogical Historical Research (IGHR) was first held at Howard College, now Samford University. It was originally named Willo Institute of Genealogy after its sponsor, Willlo Press, a local press run by Elizabeth Wood Thomas, who had the "vision to realize we need to know how to do genealogical research."[44]

Only leading researchers and scholars in the field are invited to teach IGHR courses. Initially, the institute was a two-day event involving 40 students and five faculty members. In 1965, it became a week-long residential program held in June. Director Jean Thomason doubled the number of instructors and the number of courses, and over 200 students were enrolled.[45] Currently, this institute is arguably the most prestigious of all genealogical institutes in the United States. IGHR enrolls approximately 300 students for the week-long courses each June. The courses are mostly filled to capacity within a week of opening for registration. Course enrollments are normally restricted to 25 students, as the goal is to have interaction between instructors and students. Students travel from all parts of the United States to attend the genealogical and historical classes offered during this institute.

Respondent Attendance at the IGHR

Table 8 indicates that the IGHR is the third-most-popular continuing education program among our respondents, with 20 (13.16 percent) of the respondents having attended a total of 53sessions over the past five years.

Certification and Accreditation of Genealogists

BCG and the ICAPGen

The Family History Library's Accredited Genealogist program was started in 1964, the same year as the Board for Certification of Genealogists (BCG). However, the Family History Library's program was discontinued. In August 2001, the Family and Church History Department transferred its ownership and responsibility for testing and administering the program to the International Commission for the Accreditation of Professional Genealogists (ICAPGen).

The credential Accredited Genealogist (AG) indicates that the individual has passed a proctored test and has mastered certain competencies in the field of genealogical research. A researcher must have thorough understanding in a particular specialty. When a person has more than 1,000 hours of research experience in one of the specified areas, that person may submit an application, and the accreditation process begins.[46]

The BCG

The BCG initially certified two research categories: the Certified Genealogist (CG) and the Certified Genealogical Record Searcher (CGRS). To meet the needs of various societies who wanted high-caliber speakers, the Certified Genealogical Lecturer (CGL) category was established.

In addition, the Certified Genealogical Instructor (CGI) credential was awarded to highly qualified teachers. Only two individuals met those requirements. Also, two lineage research categories were established: the Certified American Lineage Specialist (CLS) and the Certified American Indian Lineage Specialist (CAILS). These two categories were collapsed into the Certified Lineage Specialist (CLS).

On October 16, 2005, all three of the research credentials were consolidated; anyone with another BCG research credential would hold the CG credential.

The BCG also sponsors skillbuilding lectures at national conferences. The Skillbuilding Track is designed to help researchers improve their skills based on the current standards in the field.

In 2009, Skillbuilding Certification Seminars were held at both the NGS Conference in Raleigh and the FGS conference in Little Rock. These skillbuilding sessions focus on standards in the profession, which are consistently enforced.

In addition, the BCG Education Fund was established in 2000. This fund operates as an independent 501 (c)(3) charitable trust. The fund promotes the educational aims of BCG and has offered scholarships of various kinds, consistent with its mission.[47]

Certified Genealogists

According to Lynn C. McMillion, BCG Executive Director (2009), the Board has certified 990 CGs, 32 CGLs, 3 CGIs (no longer a category), 126 CLSs (no longer a category), and 7 CAILSs (no longer a category). As of April 11, 2009, 279 held the CG, and 17 held the CGL.[48]

Respondent Certification

Among the respondents in this study, eleven held CG credentials, and four held AG credentials (Tables 8 and 9).

Participants' responses reflected the upholding of standards. Regarding reasons for seeking credentials from BCG, one respondent "decided to become a professional in order to do research that was up to professional standards. It is just too easy to just pick names out of various sources without really analyzing what you're looking at. It is now easier than ever to publish or post whatever you like whether you have anything to back it up or not."

What can be said about the rigor of the certification process is best stated by William Litchman, a scientist with a Ph.D. in chemistry who went through the process. Litchman was eager to put to the test all of the skills, methods, and specialized techniques that he had learned over the years; he viewed the certification process as a challenge to apply the scientific method to the field of genealogy. He was "overwhelmed by, and excited about, the amount of attention to detail that was required." He was especially impressed at the documentation of sources, discovering that up to that time he had been "only doing what was barely adequate." He stated, "The work required for Certified Genealogist is comparable to that needed to earn a master's degree. It takes about the same length of time to put things together for certification, once you have acquired the necessary basic knowledge and research techniques, as it does to complete a master's-level research project and thesis, and involves the same rigorous standards."[49]

The Family History Library – Access to Resources

The Family History Library began in 1894, in tandem, with the Genealogical Society of Utah. The years between 1920 and 1940 can be characterized as the growth years. By 1937, the library housed over 19,000 books, building a reputation of being among the top five genealogical libraries in the country. In 2001, approximately 691,000 people visited the library, as more resources became accessible from local libraries. Visitors to the library now have leveled off over the last few years, with an annual average of 540,00 to 590,000.[50]

Federation of Genealogical Societies Linking the Genealogical Community

Another aspect of the leadership toward greater strength of the genealogical community and its resources, knowledge, and attitudes is the Federation of Genealogical Societies (FGS). The FGS was founded in 1976, and today its membership extends to more than 500 genealogical societies.

The purpose of the FGS is to link members of the genealogical community. It publishes *Forum* magazine, with articles pertaining to the management of societies and other genealogical news. It also publishes a series of *Society Strategy Papers* about operating a genealogical society. The FGS also links the genealogical community through the scheduling of its annual four-day conference, with one full day devoted to society management topics.[51]

The Association of Professional Genealogists

Launched in 1979, the Association of Professional Genealogists (APG), a non-profit association, is dedicated to promoting the awareness of, and interest in, genealogy as a profession. This association believes that exchanging information and sharing expertise among professional genealogists is an effective way to develop genealogical skills among professional researchers, writers, lecturers, teachers, librarians, and family historians who want to learn more in their professional work. There were 19 initial members.[52]

This organization grew rapidly, with members representing almost all states. In January 1986, the *APG Quarterly* evolved from the *APG Newsletter*. In January 2001, the APG Directory of Professional Genealogists became available on the Web. In 1993, the first Association Chapters were developed in New York and Salt Lake City. The purpose of the chapters is to encourage members to interact in local groups for learning. In 2007, Moody reported

24 chapters of the APG.[53] Since that time, the APG mailing list has been made available to members to encourage them to network and learn. This forum e-list offers outstanding leadership for learning by the top genealogists in the field.

In 2007, the membership of APG was over 1,800. Its growth includes approximately 100 new members per year.[54] Reflecting an international interest, membership in 2003 included individuals from Australia, Austria, Canada, England, France, Germany, Ireland, Isle of Man, Hungary, Israel, Italy, Kuwait, Netherlands, New Zealand, Poland, Romania, Scotland, Slovenia, South Africa, Sweden, and Switzerland.[55]

Genealogy and Higher Education

The past two decades have seen another movement in academia involving those who are looking for progress toward the union of the disciplines of genealogy and history, and the end of the "cold war between historians and genealogists" in higher education.[56] This researcher believes that there are more opportunities today for genealogy to become acceptable in higher education now that the theoretical framework for genealogy has been developed and the field of genealogy is legitimate as a field of study in higher education. This theoretical framework was developed by Dr. Carolyn Billingsley in her doctoral dissertation and in her subsequent book, *Communities of Kinship: Antebellum Families and the Settlement of the Cotton Frontier* (Univ. of Georgia Press, 2004*)*. This researcher believes that the whole field of genealogy will become acceptable in a very short time for the reasons discussed below. I personally believe this is a necessary future step for the field of genealogy, and I have personally become involved in developing a BA and MA in genealogical studies at Akamai University for this reason.

What Genealogists Must Do

Mills pointed out a need that still must be filled: that is, it is necessary to build a cadre of genealogical scholars who have the qualifications needed to teach genealogy in higher education.[57] She viewed the lack of qualified people as a serious handicap among genealogists. This author believes this handicap must be resolved as quickly as possible. Clearly, a need exists for university-level programs in genealogical studies. Additionally, interested genealogical scholars in related fields such as history, sociology, theology, anthropology, biology, archeology, and psychology need to move toward genealogical certification to augment their terminal degrees in their disciplines, thereby helping to build the case for the study of genealogy as an academic field.

Changing Structures in Higher Education

Through practical implementation of the genealogical field of study, it will develop its contributions and will find a niche in higher education. This researcher believes that with the Internet and the degree and variety of communication flowing in this age, genealogy will find its own place in academia--not as an adjunct to another social science but on its own and possibly as the progenitor of a whole new topical area of studies. Perhaps in a few years, many universities may want the genealogical field of studies in their topical areas of studies.

We also need to bear in mind that the structure in academia has changed over the past decade; at most universities and colleges, the old-style departments are fenced in with mental boundaries of various disciplines no longer existing. Departments have collapsed into the broader divisional structures of groupings of disciplines. Forward-moving universities and colleges now operate within divisional structures, and many operate with topical areas of studies. Disciplinary departments were the old industrial area configurations coming out of the business model, where supervisors had to watch the workers to ensure that everyone put in a day's work. Thus, fences were built as departments became territorial and department heads became "boundary maintainers." Today, we find topical areas as Social and Cultural Studies or Human Development and Family Studies.

Today's information-oriented society is leaning toward distance learning programs as more and more universities are offering undergraduate and graduate degrees. Distance education has helped to lift the old configurations into new, more fluid structures of open planning. In part, this is also a wiser use of human resources.

Now with faculty teaching in various areas, new configurations in topical areas encourage instructors to teach in a variety of areas and to develop more of their latent expertise. This change has, in part, come about with tight economic times, and it is beneficial for the instructors to develop in-house expertise in related areas. This author believes that with the Internet as a facilitator of communication about and for genealogy, expansive opportunities are available for genealogy to become a much larger force in higher education and to draw in other courses of the social sciences and natural sciences. With DNA material being acceptable under such topical areas as the development of humankind in family and community studies or health studies and the development of humankind, which include aspects of the social and natural sciences, genealogy will find its place in the academic mainstream, as archivists have already accepted genealogy as an academic discipline[57] and many historians already teach some genealogy classes.

The most important commitment for genealogists is to begin to educate the people about what professional genealogy is. Indeed, genealogy itself will be the force behind gathering together other disciplines into its fold for topical areas of studies.

New programs now underway, such as the Boston University Certificate Program in Genealogical Research and the new Bachelor and Master Degrees at Akamai University, are slowly filtering into the psyche of higher education administrators. Academia will soon be accepting genealogy as a scientific discipline because of these four developments:

1. The field now has the Billingsley theoretical framework, which legitimizes genealogy as a field of study in higher education. [58]

2. The advances, research, and written material about DNA have put genealogy high on the radar screen of the public and in higher education studies.

3. Distance education is now mainstream; the number of students taking at least one online course continues to grow at a higher rate than overall higher education enrollments.[59] Distance learning universities--especially the large for-profit ones--will become highly competitive and will want to embrace genealogical studies programs to increase their student choices of subjects and programs in broad fields of curricular areas.

4. There are more avenues to pursue as forward-moving universities are organizing many courses around topical areas within broader divisional structures. These universities have used this approach partly to encourage faculty to teach in broader areas in tight economic times, in order to keep from hiring more faculty. The competition for students among online universities will intensify, and eventually online education will have a higher enrollment than universities in fixed settings. These online universities will seek to attract more students and will recognize the growing interest in genealogical studies. Thus, universities will soon include genealogical programs.

Research Methodology

This study was an exploratory case study of the reasons why the members of a sample of a "professional genealogy group" became interested in genealogy and continued on to become professional genealogists.

The major open-ended questions asking each respondent to write a short paragraph were:

1. Why you began to study genealogy
2. Why you continued with genealogy to become a professional genealogist

To provide a framework of the respondents as genealogists and as professional genealogists, other questions were asked such as the respondent's age, number of years of involvement in genealogy, number of years as a professional genealogist, education, earned professional genealogical credentials, honorary credentials, certification (if any) and year of certification, genealogy educational certificates, continuing education and professional tasks carried out as a professional genealogist, type of books written, where genealogy classes or seminars were taught, type of affiliated work organization, number of national conferences attended over the past five years, and approximate amount of time spent in genealogy work per week.

The Questionnaire

The questionnaire was designed during February and the first week of March 2009. It was based on literature review and background knowledge. It was sent to two colleagues to review and comment on its utility and validity. Changes were made. It was then sent to another colleague for a pre-test. The cover letter was written and then given to a colleague to review.

Population and Sampling

I selected a "professional genealogy group" that was a national and international group with members listed and profiled on the World Wide Web. This group had approximately 1,800 members and an online directory of most of the members by state was available. The directory yielded profiles of 1,419 members, with not all members online. These members served as the population from which to select my sample of 200 members for this study.

Sampling Process

Each state was reviewed, and all individuals were numbered consecutively, with the ninth person tagged as a member of the sample. The number nine was selected because the total membership of 1,800 was evenly divisible by nine. As some individuals did not include their e-mail address in their profiles, I went to the next listing, and if no e-mail address was there I went on to the next name. The first wave of individuals for the sample numbered 131. Next, I shifted to a non-probability sampling procedure. I then decided to draw additional names from states that did not reflect a potential member of the sample with the consecutive numbering of every ninth one that I had used. This drawing produced six names. I then selected the next two names from each of the states with the least members selected. These states were California, Utah, Florida, and Texas.

I then asked an outside person to select a number between one and ten. This number was five. Every state list was visited again, and the numbering was continuous through the states, with every fifth person selected. Again, if the fifth one did not have an e-mail address in his or her profile, the next one on the list was selected. Once my sample list was complete, I engaged Survey Monkey, an online survey company, to administer my survey.

Case Study Sampling

Theoretically, for a case study that has the purpose of explaining phenomena, a purposive sampling strategy is appropriate for qualitative case study research.[60] It is not necessary to use a probability sampling procedure after setting criteria for the sample.[61] However, for the present study, members of every state should have a chance to be in the sample, due to the significant differences in available resources and historical religious ethos among the states (e.g., LDS in Utah). These differences would influence people's interest in studying genealogy and in becoming professional genealogists. Thus, a probability-sampling frame was selected for the beginning of the sampling procedures. Then I went back and selected from the lists on a non-probability basis, as explained.

Data Collection

The cover letter was sent to the selected sample. This letter briefly described the survey and invited the recipient to participate by responding to the online questionnaire on or after March 10 and to complete and return it by March 18, 2009. There were six permanent opt-outs that had been configured previously. I then turned to the lists and selected six more respondents from the largest representative states, moving to the next individual listed after the last selected respondent. I sent a follow-up letter on March 16, 2009. Meanwhile, I continued with my review of the literature, which I had begun in February.

On March 13, I received an email from the executive of the professional group of my selected sample indicating that the study had "strong implications" of sponsorship by the "sampled professional genealogy group," although there was no specific written statement to that effect. It was necessary that I delete questions 15, 16, and 17 from the original questionnaire. I also deleted a phrase that referred to the professional group in the cover letter.

It is important to keep in mind that the sampling procedures used and the sample size restricted any attempts to generalize from the exploratory questions and findings.

Responses

I received 91 completed questionnaires--a response rate of 46 percent. According to a University of Texas at Austin response rate analysis of the different types of surveys, online surveys with a 50 percent response rate are considered average; therefore, we can say that this response rate was about average. http://www.utexas.edu/academic/diia/assessment?lar/teaching/gather/method/survey-response.php?ask=research

Analyses

On March 19, I began to complete some of the analyses and developed the responses into tables. I contracted Fisher Statistical Services to perform cross-tabulations with their SPSS program, as I no longer had an SPSS program. At this time, I began collecting materials and sending for articles for my literature review.

On April 22, I began analysis of responses to question 4: "Why did I decide to study genealogy?" Analyses of the remainder of the questions continued through April. The analyses involved placing the paragraph responses into conceptual categories. I photocopied the paragraphs, cut up the paragraphs, and stapled the question response paragraphs into appropriate category folders with the sheet of the individual respondent's responses in each category in order to relate the response to the previous question response. As I completed the analysis of the responses to the questionnaire, I returned to the literature review and developed the model of the Professional Genealogist.

Throughout May, I continued the analyses of responses to the question "Why did I become a Professional Genealogist?" and the paragraphs developing the categories for the responses and my analyses, as well as developing my Literature Review for the Background to the Study.

I then began the analysis of responses to the remainder of the questions and developed the tables displaying the data. During June, I worked on the conclusions, report, and model of the professionalization of genealogists. In July, I edited the paper and sent it to several colleagues for review.

Years Involved In Genealogy

As previously discussed, there were no clear answers to the question of why people start to study genealogy. Many journalists and writers have attributed the current surging interest in genealogy to the increase of resources on the Internet and to the popularity of the miniseries *Roots*.

I was interested in determining how long the respondents in my sample had been interested in genealogy. While the figures spread out from less than one year to more than 35 years, it can be seen in Table 1 that the largest group of respondents (27. 7 percent) had been interested in genealogy for more than 35 years. Viewing Table 1 from a larger group determination, it can be seen that 71 persons had been interested in genealogy from 16 to more than 35, while the lower numbers indicated less than 10 percent in each five-year span.

Table 1.Number of Years Involved in Genealogy

Years	Number	Percent %
Less than 1	1	1.1
1 to 5	0	0.0
6 to 9	2	2.2
7 to 10	7	7.8
11 to 15	10	11.1
16 to 20	16	17.8
21 to 26	14	15.6
27 to 35	16	17.8
More than 35 years	25	27.7
Total	91	

N = 91

Next, I asked the respondents about their age, as I felt that was important for my analyses of reasons given for studying genealogy, continuing education, and work performed as professional genealogists.

Age of Professional Genealogists

Table 2. Age of Respondents

AGE OF RESPONDENT	RESPONSE COUNT	PERCENT %
Under 30	2	2.2
31 to 40	4	4.4
41 to 50	14	15.6
51 to 60	30	33.3
61 to 70	31	34. 4
71 to 80	6	6.7
Over 80	3	3.3
Total	90	100

$N = 90$

It can be seen in Table 2 that 61 (approximately 67 percent) of the respondents were 51 to 70 years old. Three of the respondents were over 80 years old.

Why I Became Interested In Genealogy

The next question asked the respondents to indicate the main reason for their interest in genealogy. Thirty-seven responded to the forced choice, and 54 respondents wrote in "Other." These "Other" responses were categorized and used in the development of categories for responses of the paragraphs that asked the respondent to elaborate on their responses.

Table 3. Why I Became Interested in Genealogy

Response	Responses	Percent %
* A close relative had many antiques, artifacts, and old papers that fascinated me.	21	23.3
* My parents were divorced and I did not know one of them, or any of the family.	1	1.1
* Someone I knew was tracing his/her family tree and I found it fascinating.	0	0.0
* A close relative was tracing his/her family lineage and I saw how interesting it was.	6	6.7
* My spouse was tracing his/her family lineage.	2	2.2
* A teacher or professor inspired me by telling the class stories about ancestors.	1	1.1

* In school we were assigned a project/after school youth activity in genealogy.	4	4.4
* A parent died when I was very young, and I wanted to know more about my ancestors.	2	2.2
* I was adopted and wanted to find my birth parents and kinfolk.	0	0.0
* We moved so much that I did not know my kin.	0	0.0
* I was fascinated with the family databases on the World Wide Web.	0	0.0
Total	**37**	**0.19**
Other	**54**	**59.3**
Friendship		
* ___, A retired librarian of the _____ County Library was receiving requests for ancestors who had lived and died in the ___ Region and was a very good friend of my wife and myself.		
* A friend's research interest and unproven family stories		
Total	**2**	
Death/Divorce –Family fragmentation		
* My grandparents had been divorced, so I knew nothing of my paternal grandfather.		

* Death of my last living grandparent inspired me to research and pass on knowledge of the family heritage.		
* Father's paternal side all died young and it was three generations of single males. I wanted to learn more about that branch of the family.		
Total	**3**	
Religion		
* My son had a Bar Mitzvah project.		
* As a new convert to the Church of Jesus Christ of Latter-day Saints, I was encouraged to do so.		
* I'm LDS and was bitten by the genealogy bug when I was in my early 20s because of the stories about my ancestors.		
Total	**3**	
Work-Related		
* I worked at the historical society and answering genealogical queries became part of my job.		
* I worked with a "professional genealogy group" to develop and maintain it for many years. Other than that, I have not done any actual genealogical work.		
* I was a _(title of position)_ on the miniseries _Roots: The Next Generations._		

* Helped to settle kinship issues for a probate matter and was encouraged/professionally referred by the Court where my 1st affidavit of due diligence and heirship was submitted.		
Total	**4**	
History-Related		
* Civil War Business. History/ Genealogy-related		
* The *Roots* miniseries and book * The *Roots* miniseries		
* Have always loved history, and family history seemed the ultimate in "story power."		
* My training is in history, and genealogy is closely related.		
* Fascination with history and wanted to know where my ancestors/family fit in to history.		
Total	**6**	
College Work		
* A suggestion to study it in college.		
* Learning about manuscript census records in a graduate history class inspired me to look up my own family.		

* I was given a class assignment to interview a family member. I was 14. I interviewed my Dad, who showed me a few documents. He died two months later. I started asking questions of grandparents and great-aunts and uncles.		
Total	**3**	
Family		
* Never discussed family when I was a child.		
* My mother had always read historical articles to me as a young child. I became fascinated with the past, and, when reaching my 20s, I decided to trace my heritage.		
* My parents were tracing their lineage and I wanted to trace my husband's family.		
* My father was interested and I became involved to please him, but was very soon pleasing myself.		
* My mother tried to prove a lineage to a Revolutionary War ancestor, but died before she could. I did prove it to ten of them.		
* My elder son saw a notice about a ___Genealogy Conference and suggested I get a computer software program to do our family and he would help me.		

* On a vacation trip Mom asked Dad about his family. Dad said, "My grandfather's name was John and that's all I know." We detoured the archives in ____, ___ and spent the rest of the vacation there. Since then, it has been like an obsession.		
Total	7	
Kin Interested in and Doing Genealogy		
* A close relative took me to see the old family burial ground and places where my grandmother grew up.		
* Grandfather told me about a person with our surname who was a murderer, horse thief, etc., in the West. I had to find out about the family connections.		
* I started asking my maternal grandparents for stories about when they were young, and periodically asked my mother for more history until I got a little older and could do searching for myself.		
* My grandfather had a "family book" that traced his surname from 1774 to him. As a 10-year-old, I wanted to know if my ancestor born in 1774 was affected by the Revolution. I later learned that his father died as a soldier in that war, so the answer was, yes, the revolution did affect him (and me).		

* My maternal grandparents were children in the Indian Territory near Tulsa, OK, and I was always interested in the history of our family.		
* My grandmother had moved away from family once she married and had asked me to help find that side of her family that she had lost contact with.		
* My parents, grandparents, and some siblings always had some interest in family history/genealogy.		
* My grandmother spent many years doing family history research, and I followed in her footsteps.		
Total	**8**	
I Wanted to Know		
* I simply wanted to know more about my ancestors.		
* I wanted to know more about both lines of my family before my elders were gone.		
* My grandfather was 94, and I wanted to trace his lineage before he died at 97 years of age. He also had a distant cousin that had done a lot of work on his line and I just had to finish my grandfather's line. I did that and took it back about 250 years in England.		

*	I think I was born with the curiosity about my ancestor--nothing really started me questioning--I just questioned.		
*	I just wanted to know my family. I was the only one at the time to do genealogy in the family.		
*	I have always been interested in my family background.		
*	To find facts that my dad was not telling me about our family.		
*	I started in an attempt to prove that every person in the world with my surname is related to me.		
*	I had just had my first child and we had a family reunion planned. I wanted to find out more about the family to pass on to my son and to share with everyone at the reunion.		
*	I wanted to learn more about my ancestors.		
*	Became interested in family gathered at a family reunion.		
*	Found a series of newsletters written by an ancestor in the N.Y. City Library while on holiday.		
*	Family letters from the 1880s; I wanted to know who these people were and who they were talking about.		
*	Curious about my unusual surname and my heritage.		

* I had an innate interest in my ancestors.		
* Wanted to solve all the relationships for a big family reunion of near and distant cousins. Got hooked, stayed hooked.		
* My mother's family had been traced back to the Middle Ages, but we only knew my great-grandparents on my father's side.		
Total	17	
Terminology	1	
I believe the term genealogy is obsolete and should be replaced by the term Family History. FH includes genealogy and a whole lot more.		
	18	
Total 37+54=91		

$N = 91$

Why I Began To Study Genealogy

While I was interested in the major question of why the respondents began to study genealogy and why they became professionals, I also asked other general questions: number of years involved in genealogy, age, number of years as a professional genealogist, education (including genealogical credentials), years of certification, honorary genealogical credentials, educational certificates and continuing education experiences, type of tasks performed as professional genealogists, national conferences attended, and time spent on genealogical work per week.

Why did You Begin to Study Genealogy.?

Respondents were asked to elaborate in detail why they began to study genealogy as a detailed elaboration to their response to question 3. Fictional names were inserted in the examples for specific names and places that would identify the respondents.

I. The category of Kinfolk-Inspired, which received 37 (40.4 percent) of the 86 responses, was the reason the greatest number of respondents were stimulated to study genealogy. The 86 short-paragraph responses of why respondents began to study genealogy were grouped into nine categories. Five respondents did not respond to the question.

Table 4. Categories of Why I Began to Study Genealogy

Number of Category	Title of Category	Number of Responses	Percent (%)
I	Kinfolk-Inspired	37	43.4
II	Just Wanted to Know--Curious	12	13.9
III	Business/Career/Job-related	9	9.55
IV	School/College/Church Assignment Project	7	8
V	Religion	5	5
VI	Fascination with History	5	5
VII	Family Help/No Information	5	5
VIII	Friends Helping Friends	3	3
IX	Family/Fragmentation/Death/Divorce	3	3
Total		77	

N = 86 (Five did not respond.)

The kinfolk who inspired the respondents were of different relations: great-aunt, grandmother, grandfather, and great-grandfather. Fourteen responses indicated the influence of those who referred to memories of childhood and stories that kinfolk told, records they had, letters respondents found, and actions of their kinfolk.

One underlying emotion that ran throughout the responses was enthusiasm and passion for genealogical research. Also prevalent was a fascination with what their kinfolk were doing as they set the stage for the respondents to continue with the family history and family traditions, such as keeping records, keeping family relationships foremost in the center of family interactions, and collecting material things of their ancestors, including photographs. One respondent indicated that keeping the family history came with the marriage.

These paragraphs made it clear that these families were passionate about their traditions and family stories, their artifacts, and the person designated as the "genealogist." Indeed, these responses described a lifestyle or a "way of life."

Several respondents indicated that it was a family tradition to have a genealogist or a family member who kept records and documents. One aunt or grandmother kept family records over the generations. A few respondents had a query or a conflict about something said about their family history that inspired them to take up the research. Some samples from the paragraphs are written below.

◆   ◆   ◆

"It [doing genealogy] is just something my family has always been interested in–both my mother's family and my father's family. In addition, my husband's mother is known as the family genealogist in that family. So when my husband and I were married more than 40 years ago, an interest in family history came along with the marriage. My mother's aunt was the first serious genealogist I ever knew, and she was careful about sharing information until she was sure of its accuracy. She didn't document her work, except for mentioning her source in the text of her writing, but she didn't write it if she wasn't sure of it."

◆   ◆   ◆

Another respondent had "letters from my second great-grandfather, written in the 1880s to his son, my great-grandfather, which mentioned many family members and their ancestry another three generations back. I wanted to locate records on these people to learn more about them, residences and ways of life, who they were and what they were talking about them. I was also told I took after this line of the family in my likes, looks and eating habits, so, of course, I was curious."

◆   ◆   ◆

"As I answered questions resolving relationships between us many cousins, I became interested in the documentation of conflicting facts, leading me into courthouses, church records, and vital records research.

I discovered records of the social history of the ancestors (homestead record, military records); I became interested in developing the stories of their lives with documentation. Also, documentation refuted and verified old family stories to varying degrees. It was a satisfying experience to base my conclusions on documentation, not family memory nor story."

◆   ◆   ◆

"My great-aunt had compiled an extensive history of one branch of the family, and my mother had college papers from her study of her parents' families. These were both available to me at about the time of *Roots*. I then discovered that a collection of about 150 letters (1838-1880), salvaged from a trunk in grandmother's barn, included a ca. 1815 document showing a major error in the 'established line reflected in my mother's college work.' The search was on."

◆   ◆   ◆

These respondents are referring to goals beyond the material possessions of enjoyment toward higher living cultural familial goals in ways that Csikszentmihalyi and Rochberg-Halton in *The Meaning of Things* addressed as they urgently maintained, "There is an urgent need to develop vital cultural practices–ways of living that have the potential for long-term growth. We need to cultivate those objects, activities and environments that can inspire the fullest unfolding of human potential now and in the future. Patterns of meaning that do not have a self-destructive exhaustion of physical and psychic are resources built into them."[62]

Csikszentmihalyi and Rochberg-Halton continued:

> The goals one can create are not all at the same level but can range on a continuum and increasing synthetic power or generalisability. At the lower end, the goal is to prove one's individual existence, one's control over the environment. At this level, flow joins the elements of one's self into an active participation with a domain of challenges. Toys, sports equipment, books, tools, musical instruments are some of the concrete signs through which this goal may be achieved. The next level is usually one in which the self grows to include--and be included in--the network of relationships.[63]
>
> Here the goal expands from seeking rewards to one's own intentions to finding meaning in rewards obtained by others. The self expands to the social level and one's ability to enjoy is increased by being able to share the enjoyment of others.
>
> Now the possibilities for meaningful action expand geometrically, as do the opportunities of experiencing perception and flow. Motivated by a broad, enduring set of goals, the self is no longer dominated by the needs that have shaped it thus far. It can take on the challenges and responsibilities of freedom and use meaning to fashion a new world in which to live.[64]

People purchase expensive boats, planes, and equipment for hiking, and enjoy the domination of their control over their environment and all of its exhaustions; yet so simple it is that they can develop their growth of self to enjoy the happiness of others.

In the first category of "Kinfolk-Inspired" were 14 responses that mentioned childhood years and their kinfolk or their "Journeys from Childhood." Many of the respondents described with passion their memories of a relative helping them with family history or the stories told by grandparents. The emphasis was on kinfolk and family relationships, and visiting historical places; the respondent paid close attention to stories when young, hoping to be able to add some stories later in life. On the other side was the respondent who stated that while she was a child, they never discussed family.

◆   ◆   ◆

One respondent stated, "Growing up in an antebellum house with a mother who loved 'old' things, I found it fascinating to learn about people who lived before me. Two such persons pushed me toward genealogy: My maternal grandmother's mother, for whom I was supposedly named, and my paternal grandfather's grandfather, who supposedly was the first minister of the rural church that was the center of my family's life. The kicker was the trunk my grandmother, at momma's request, uncovered beneath a pile of boxes and old quilts.… It was filled with pieces and pieces of paper from the 1800s, all pertaining to my grandmothers-in-law. The county they lived in had endured two courthouse fires, and many of these papers would have been lost. I was a hopeless genealogist from that point on."

◆   ◆   ◆

"My grandmother fascinated me with her stories of picking beans, no electricity or plumbing. Yet there were a lot of conversations, photos and visits with friends and family much older than myself. Family relationships were stressed while I was growing up. I paid close attention hoping to pass along this information some day and being able to add my own adventures to the family collection. I began documenting to preserve the memories of these incredible spirits. Time changes so quickly and today's events become yesterday's history overnight!"

◆   ◆   ◆

"My love for genealogy was formed at a young age. I had a number of great-aunts who would write down our family's history, and I always enjoyed reading these. After I married my husband, my mother-in-law would point out all of her cherished possessions that were passed down through generations. She also knew her family genealogy off the top of her head. I decided to start doing genealogy on my own as a way to write down my husband's family genealogy information. This seemingly small venture opened up a whole new interesting world to me. Since this project, I have grown in my desire to learn more about the field of genealogy and a desire to work at a higher level of professionalism."

◆   ◆   ◆

"My mother's parents migrated as pioneer children to the Indian Territory in 1897. I was always interested in why their parents moved and how people lived in the Midwest during the 19th century. My interest was stimulated because my parents took us to museums, historical sites, and antique shops while I was growing up."

◆   ◆   ◆

II. Just Wanted to Know, Curious About My Ancestors (twelve responses)

Some respondents had heard stories about their ancestors and wanted to find out if they were true.

"When I held different family heirlooms, I felt a closeness to the people who had used that tool or to the babies who had sat in that toddler seat. I saw similarities in our faces when I looked at old photographs. I thought about how these people lived and died and I knew nothing more than their names and pertinent dates, if that much. It was sad to think that these people had lived, worked, loved, laughed and cried but were gone from my family's memories. I wanted to research them and make them more real for my present family members. I also wanted to research my husband's ancestors so that our children could understand both their northern and southern heritage. Once I started the research, I found that my personality was well suited for the 'treasure hunt' aspect of genealogy."

◆   ◆   ◆

"Mine was the fairly common story of a descent from someone on the Mayflower. I pursued it because I wanted to know more about it. As I continued the study, I found that it was not true."

◆   ◆   ◆

"When I was in my early 20s, I began doing genealogy in earnest, trying to track down relatives with unusual surnames. As I had time, and with encouragement from my mother, I gradually put more pieces of the family history together. I found out that family histories, oral and written, were not necessarily accurate and that I could find out things from public records that people didn't really want dug up. I also discovered in myself an interest in doing research and a need to satisfy curiosity."

◆   ◆   ◆

"From the moment that I rolled my first census microfilm through the reader and found (De De Dye) ___ ____ in 1850, ____ County, _____, that was it for me. I was a hobbyist for very many years and began the educational track two or three years ago. I have attended IGHR, NIGR, am a member of the original Pro Gen Study Group, and am completing the 16th and final lesson of the NGS course. I love the aspect that I think of as micro-history. Writing the stories of ordinary people against their historical backdrop. Digging out the tiniest details about their lives and movements."

◆   ◆   ◆

"My dad told so many not-so-true stories about my family and I had to find out the facts. Most everything he stated was not factual about whom he was talking, but more him not them. Found out he was the black sheep in the family."

◆   ◆   ◆

"I have an interesting heritage. Dad's father was a white sharecropper. He came from a long line of former horse breeders, and a confederate cavalryman. Knowing that made me want to dig deeper into that side of the family. My mother's grandfather was a New York Quaker whose ancestors ran the Underground Railroad. He married a Southern belle. I wanted to know why, and about their ancestry. Mom's mother is a cousin of Gene Autry, so I wanted to find the connection. When I got married, I immediately dug up my wife's family to give her the same sense of grounding in American history and heritage that I had. Now, I do it for my friends."

◆   ◆   ◆

"I just had my first child and we had a family reunion planned. I wanted to find out more about the family to pass on to my son and to share with everyone at the reunion. I quit my job after the birth of my first child and had some time on my hands. I lived in Los Angeles and had heard about the LDS family research centers so I went to check it out."

◆   ◆   ◆

III. Business, Career, and Job Skills-Related (nine responses)

In this category are the responses of those who indicated that their educational field involved skills that were immediately transferable to the genealogical research field, their career was related to genealogy, or they had a business involving genealogical products. Respondents included a lawyer, a librarian, a person who did TV work with the producer of *Roots,* an engineer, a person who traveled with the U.S. Defense Department, and one who was in the Civil War book business.

"I was a history teacher. I also used genealogy in my classes to get students interested in history via their own families."

◆   ◆   ◆

"There were ambiguous and contradictory oral family traditions for both my maternal and paternal lines, and I wanted to test the elements of each for authenticity or fancy. Both my mother and my father labored for years attempting to document their respective family lines. As a lawyer, my strong suits were deep research and documentation for trial and appellate briefs, so the pursuit of genealogical records was a natural fit for me."

◆   ◆   ◆

"My field of interest required a high level of research expertise; I helped to settle kinship issues for a probate matter and was encouraged/professionally referred by the court where my 1st affidavit of due diligence and heirship was submitted."

"Worked at a historical society and answering genealogical queries became part of my job. I have always loved doing social history research."

◆   ◆   ◆

"My education was in engineering, and problem solving was a natural activity. When I found I could solve family history and genealogy problems using original source materials, it seemed natural to do so. Written analysis and presentation of results also came easily and made the results more interesting, more useful and more lasting as well."

◆   ◆   ◆

"I was a __(member of the team) of the TV production of *Roots*, and meeting and talking with Alex Haley and filming the story of his ancestors inspired me to find out more about my own and to try to write some of my own history. Although I was a second-(paternal) and third-generation (maternal) Czech-American, our family still maintained many cultural traditions. And I was interested in finding more about my heritage."

IV. School/College or Church Assignment or Class Project in Genealogy (seven responses)

For some respondents, the stimulation came from a class assignment or project in school or college work, which led them to continue with the study of genealogy and family history. Their responses conveyed the power of those assignments and the resulting interactions, and how they motivated the respondents to continue on with the study of genealogy.

"The English lit teacher assigned *Ivanhoe*. Afterward, we were to prepare a family chart and a coat of arms (unless our family had one). One of the wealthy families had their family tree and crest all the way back to England, and then some. I was so intrigued and somewhat envious. I thought *I can do that*. Oh, how innocent I was. But I was determined; I've made it to England and to France on both my parents' lines, as well as on my husband's line."

◆   ◆   ◆

"When I was 14, I had the opportunity to take what was called a Book of Remembrance class associated with my church. We were given assignments such as filling out pedigree charts, gathering pictures and short life histories from parents and grandparents. All of my family were helpful and encouraged me. Some of the things I collected so many years ago are now family treasures. I found the study fascinating and compelling then and now."

◆   ◆   ◆

"My Oregon History professor was teaching us about the Oregon Trail migration and kept telling us personal stories about his ancestors' experiences on the trail. All I could think about was how I wanted to know those kinds of things about my own ancestors. That prompted me to start researching."

◆   ◆   ◆

"When I was in college, I took a class on North American Genealogical Research. I began looking for my father's ancestors, and had pretty good success. After that, I was hooked."

◆　　　　◆　　　　◆

"It was a family tree project in my home economics class that started my interest in Genealogy."

V. Religion (five responses)

Religious beliefs drew five responses, as some of the respondents had religious beliefs that they should know about their ancestors. One respondent stated, "We believe that families have a role that extends beyond this mortal life. Thus, they are very important to us."

◆　　　　◆　　　　◆

"My religious beliefs include family history work (as did my grandmother's). I am continuing what she started as part of my responsibility to my ancestors."

◆　　　　◆　　　　◆

"In my church, I was given a blessing with the suggestion to study family history while in school. I was attending BYU at the time, and so I thought I would just take a beginning family history class and call it good. I ended up loving it and went on to major in family history and became a professional genealogist."

◆　　　　◆　　　　◆

"My son was required to do a project. I was delegated to help him. He had been doing grandparent interviewing in his school, so we decided to do a family tree with him. After the Bar Mitzvah, he stopped but I was hooked."

◆　　　　◆　　　　◆

"I am LDS and was bitten by the genealogy bug when I was in my early 20s because of the stories about my ancestors. I heard many stories about how my ancestors were members of handcarts coming west and the hardships they willingly endured."

VI. Fascination with History (five responses)

Five responses expressed a love and interest in history above all, which was foremost in these respondents' pursuit of genealogical studies.

◆   ◆   ◆

"I have always found the personal stories in history to be fascinating—not just the stories of famous/important people, but more often the stories of 'ordinary folk.' So, as a young mother looking for something to fill my creative urges, I began researching my own ancestors to learn about their lives and the times they lived in. I took classes in genealogy, family history, and writing whenever possible but had to learn mostly just by doing research until my children were grown. Then, about 6-7 years ago, I went back to college and graduated in 2004 from BYU with a degree in Family History. Now in my own research, and as I teach others about family history, I concentrate on finding the stories—both amazing and hum dum—about the people that came together in our history to create who we are today."

◆   ◆   ◆

"I was interested in, and a student of, history from childhood. This extended to my family, but it went far beyond that. When I settled in my current town, I become involved in the local historical society. Local history and genealogy are inseparable.

The summer after I read *Roots* as a teenager, we visited the Family History Library in Salt Lake City on a vacation out West, and I found my grandmother in the 1905 census when she was five years old. That was all it took."

◆   ◆   ◆

"Working on a master's degree in public history with the intention of working at a historic site, I began to use the local history resources to research my own family history."

◆   ◆   ◆

"My father had his grandfather's Civil War scrapbook and family Bible. I have always been interested in history and studied anthropology in college and graduate schools. The combination of history and anthropology is genealogy."

VII. Family Help or No Information from Family (five responses)

There were five responses in this category, and one respondent said that she did not know anything at all because when she was young, family was never discussed.

◆   ◆   ◆

"I wanted to do a family tree for my child and did not know anything at all about my ancestors."

◆   ◆   ◆

"My mother had always read historical articles to me as a young child. I became fascinated with 'the past' and, when reaching my 20s, decided to trace my heritage. I feel that there are many people who just have a native interest in 'those that came before.' Still others become interested when they start again due to the realization of the brevity of life.... We are all a product of all the ancestors that went before. To realize that we have to inherit blue eyes from both parents (even though both parents might have brown eyes) helped me know that my 2ⁿᵈ great-grandfather was not full-blood Cherokee as the rolls stated, but had 'white' from both sides."

◆   ◆   ◆

"I remember clearly asking my father about his ancestry when I was about 15—he took me to a local historical society to look for books on the family name (he had no idea how to do family research and, in fact, was not interested but was willing to try to point me in a direction). When I went to college, I chose Utah (I was from New Jersey) for the mountains and change of scenery, but a great advantage was the old genealogy library—it gradually took off from there."

◆   ◆   ◆

"While on a vacation, my husband and I visited a college where several of his ancestors had studied, and we were able to find information about his family in their library. His family stories were so interesting that I found myself wanting to learn about my own ancestry. Despite having some written information on one of my mother's ancestral lines, my parents had little knowledge about the origins of our family. When I began my own research, I was able to use the Web to locate and meet a 92-year-old cousin (now 97) who had many interesting stories to share about our family. Once I met her, I was hooked on genealogy!"

◆   ◆   ◆

"My elder son saw a notice about a ____ Genealogy Conference and suggested I get a computer software program to do our family and he would help me.

However, when I actually started contacting our family members and really started researching all sides of our family, especially after I took a Beginner's Course thanks to the ____ Genealogical Society of ____, he then thought I had gone out of control. From this beginning, initially at my son's behest, it wasn't long before I branched out into doing research for others."

VIII. Friends Helping Friends (three responses)

While only three respondents fit in this category, they gave excellent examples of how groups or teams bound with the strength of mutually shared goals can accomplish a great deal.

"I started in an attempt to prove that every person in the world with my surname is related to me.

I received a letter from a man in ____ that gave me the names and addresses of every person with my surname in the ___ telephone book. I sent 11 letters asking 'Are we related? Tell me about your family history.' These letters created a need for additional research or included names of other people to contact. Within four years, I have traced our mutual ancestry to the progenitor of the family who was a merchant in ____ in the first half of the 19th century. Today, the family tree includes more than 1,700 descendants of this man and his two wives."

◆   ◆   ◆

"(Jennie) had been researching tombstone inscriptions of the area for the earliest records that were not available from any known public record. The iron industry had long since faded away and families had migrated westward. With her help and others, we assisted in obtaining those inscriptions and organized the local chapter of the ____ County Genealogical Society as part of the ____ Genealogical Society. I was conversant with the new age of computers, so, as a project, we began to self-publish a number of those early records. The first county census of 1820 was the start."

◆   ◆   ◆

"A friend was reading quarterlies at work during her breaks and I became interested in them. My grandmother said her grandmother's husband died in the Civil War. Well, then, why are there medical bills from 1876? This is a still unresearched personal query."

◆   ◆   ◆

IX. Family Fragmentation, Death/Divorce (three responses)

Three responses were relevant to this category. One respondent's parents were divorced; another respondent's father had died at an early age; and another's last living grandparent had died. These events prompted the respondents to study genealogy.

"My parents were divorced, and I did not know one of them, nor any of the family. My father had left when I was eight years old, plus he never spoke of his family, preferring to act as if they didn't exist; therefore, I hardly knew of one side of my family. I wanted to know about them and more about my mother's family and to feel as if I didn't just pop out of nowhere, so I began to research my personal history of the family."

◆   ◆   ◆

"My father was a submariner in the Pacific in WWII. He came home from the war and died of tuberculosis. He died in January. I was born in May. I never knew him; by the time I was old enough to ask, most of my grandparents were already gone. My appetite to know my genealogy became insatiable. Now, I do genealogy for others on a regular basis, and I have the same passion for it as the first day I started. Love history, love genealogy, love research and love digging for the truth."

◆   ◆   ◆

"The death of my last living grandparent inspired me to research and pass on knowledge of the family heritage to my children. I have a business in _____ and heard about the library there dedicated to family history. I visited in 1996 and was impressed with their holdings and introductory classes and volunteers willing to help. I collected basic family information from interviewing my parents and extended family and then found my parents' families in the 1920 census and was hooked from then on."

Why I Became A Professional Genealogist

Respondents were asked to select their main reason for continuing with genealogy to become a professional genealogist. Eighty-nine respondents answered the question, and two did not respond. As with question no. 4, forced-choice responses were used within the categories for the next question, which asked them to write a paragraph elaborating on why they decided to become professional genealogists.

Table 5. Reasons Why I Became a Professional Genealogist Main Reason

Response	No.	Percent (%)
* I wanted to help others with their work in genealogy.	15	16.8
* I wanted to continue to learn and develop my skills and knowledge in the field.	18	20
* The increasing availability of research resources and the Internet made the transition possible.	1	.01
* The analytical work and puzzles in finding people were so interesting that I wanted to continue to develop my skills as a professional.	40	44.9

* I needed a source of income based on previous education and experience .	5	.05
Total	79	
Other (please specify)	10	
Total	89	
Other		
* I continued to assist with a number of other publications. Having done so, my wife at the time now was interested in societies that made it a policy for documented ancestral lineages. Since I had technical and research experience and since we both had a common ancestor from the Rev. War, it was a mutual experience. We were excited to travel widely over Ohio, West Virginia, Pennsylvania, Kentucky, and North Carolina to research our roots and to collect the		
documentation and publications in this effort.		
* Might as well share my abilities and resources with others as I enjoy the chase.		

* I wanted to convert my amateur interest in genealogy into a part-time career after retirement from my day job.		
* I wanted to make money doing what I love.		
* A combination of most of the above.		
* Too bad I can't select more than one reason. But my family's research was so difficult I felt that any client's work would be a walk in the park--it was and has been through over 200 clients.		
* I have not yet decided whether to become a professional genealogist. I am an___ member for the professionalism I can apply to my own work.		
* Essentially all of the above, save only the current need for an additional source of income.		
* I felt my ethnic group has been underserved because of the ___, __, and language barriers.		
* I became a librarian.		

N = 89

As Table 5 indicates, 40 (44.9 percent) of the 89 respondents indicated that analytical work and puzzles in finding people were the main reason they wanted to become professional genealogists. Consistent with that response was their desire to continue to learn more and to develop their skills and knowledge in the field of genealogy. Fifteen (16.8 percent) of the respondents wanted to help others with their work in genealogy. There were ten "other" responses.

Respondents were then asked to write a paragraph elaborating on their response to the previous question, "Why did you decide to become a professional genealogist?" Eighty-two responded; nine did not answer the question.

Two copies of these pages of collated paragraphs were printed. One set of copies was cut up and stapled into folders of the created category of response. In the folders of categorical response with the page of each individual's response to Question 6, "Why did you decide to become a professional genealogist?" was placed into the categorical folder with the analyzed paragraph.

Table 6. Categories of Why Reasons Why I Decided to Become A Professional Genealogist

Category	Title of Category	No. of Responses	Percent (%)
I	Continue to Expand Skills and Learn More	22	26.8
II	Wanted to Help Others	18	21.9
III	Loved Puzzles and Challenges	18	21.9
IV	Career/Job/Transfer of Skills	13	15.8
V	Looking toward a Productive Retirement	10	12.1
VI	Increasing Availability of Resources on Internet	1	.01
Total		82	

N = 82

I. Continue to Expand Skills and Learn More

No significant differences were found among the respondents' reasons for wanting to become professional genealogists. Without a doubt, the respondents wanted to learn how to do genealogical research the correct way, meeting the standards of the profession, and they wanted to continue their education and their learning. One might also say that the professional associations' emphasis on standards and knowledge and the leadership in these organizations, exemplified in their continuing sponsorship of seminars and institutes, impressed upon professional genealogists that the correct methods and modes of working are critical signs of a professional genealogist. Underlying the responses is the desire "to learn how to do genealogy and genealogical research the correct way and not be seen as one who just copies down any data as correct."

Twenty-two (26.8 percent) of the respondents indicated that they wanted to continue to expand their skills and knowledge. These responses reflect Abraham Maslow's Theory of the Hierarchy of Human Motivation (Figure 1).[65] Maslow's theory states that needs are important in motivating human behavior.

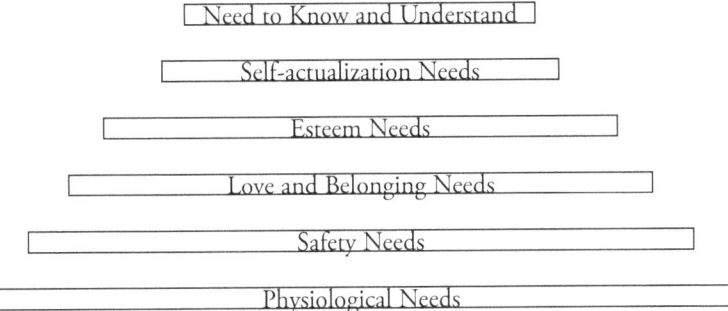

Figure 1: Maslow's Hierarchy and Prepotency of Needs

The order is important: each need is built on the ones below. Physiological needs are necessary to maintain life: food, water, oxygen, and rest. Once the physiological needs are satisfied, the next needs that emerge are safety. These safety needs for children and adults are demonstrated by a need for order or routine, and withdrawal from strange and unfamiliar situations. Love is a desire for affectionate relations with people and for a place in the group of people. Esteem needs are recognition needs—the need to be a worthwhile person to others, resulting in confidence, strength, and usefulness. When such needs are thwarted, a person feels inferior and helpless.

The self-actualization need is the need "to become the person one can be" or to become the person in life befitting his or her potential. This need is satisfied when one becomes what he or she wants to become (e.g., a good teacher, a good doctor, a good nurse, or a good engineer). The individuals in whom these needs have been generally satisfied are considered the healthiest people in society.

Maslow was uncertain that the desires to know and to understand—cognitive needs—we're as clearly established in all human beings as were the others. Although curiosity, exploration and the desire to acquire further knowledge can be readily observed, they are more evident in persons of higher intelligence than in those of lower intelligence. [66]

It is also important to note that a reversal of the order of needs may occur. In today's economy, many people have lost their jobs and homes, and may be living in tents, with physiological and safety needs demanding their total attention.

Maslow stated, "In examining self-actualizing people directly, I find that in all cases, at least in our culture, they are dedicated people, devoted to some task 'outside themselves,' some vocation, or duty, or beloved job. Generally the devotion and dedication is so marked that one can fairly use the old words vocation, calling, or mission to describe their passionate, selfless, and profound feeling for their 'work.'"[67]

In this study, some responses reflected self-actualization needs, and the need to know and to understand.

"I decided to become a professional in order to do research that was up to professional standards. It is too easy to just pick names out of various sources without really analyzing what you're looking at. It is now easier than ever to publish/post whatever you like, whether you have anything to back it up or not."

◆   ◆   ◆

"I wanted to learn to establish and record who the families were, how they lived, who were their neighbors, what events affected their lives, what were these people like. To do this I discovered I must be methodological in my research and data collection and analysis. I could not 'collect names.' I came to understand the need for all professional genealogists to build strong cases, by creating a proof argument in writing to allow your argument to be tested by others. The peer review is a must if the argument is to be considered a strong valid statement of what happened."

◆   ◆   ◆

"I am continuing to learn and to develop my skills. I want the work I leave for future generations to reflect skill and knowledge in the field, as well as to be interesting."

◆   ◆   ◆

"After years of working on my own family, I decided I wanted to be better trained, so I returned to school where I subsequently got an associate degree in genealogy, then a bachelor's degree in community and family history, ultimately a master's in American history."

◆   ◆   ◆

"I wanted to develop my skills by attending genealogy-related training courses and to become involved in organizations to meet other people with interests similar to mine."

◆   ◆   ◆

"The fellow members of the 'professional groups' and fellow professionals who follow high standards set a high standard from which I learned and elevated my own practices."

II. Wanted to Help Others

Wanting to help others received 18 (21.9 percent) of the responses. These respondents experienced joy in helping others learn how to find their ancestors. Csikszentmihalyi and Rochberg-Halton described finding such satisfaction through toys, sports equipment, books, tools, and musical instruments: dominance and control goals can be achieved through such things. However, through goals at a higher level, the self grows to include--and be included--in the network of family relationships. These goals grow from seeking rewards to one's own intentions to a more "social" level and the ability to share the enjoyment of others.[68]

In Maslow's hierarchy of human needs, examples of this category of responses also exemplify the "self-actualization level of being."

◆   ◆   ◆

"I have a desire to share my knowledge of family history and genealogy with others because I know the joy it has brought to me—really making me a more well-rounded person. I feel a desire to know who and where we have come from is basic in most people. As we learn about our ancestors and the lives they led, we can be better people ourselves and develop a sense of gratitude for them."

◆   ◆   ◆

"I really enjoy teaching others how to do their own genealogy and seeing that wonderful light in their eyes when they find their first person on their own and when they have solved an especially difficult research problem."

◆   ◆   ◆

"I love it so much and love to help other people discover the thrill of finding out who the people were that came before them."

◆   ◆   ◆

"I want to help others preserve their family memories. To find, organize, and discover the most accurate and credible truth of history on a very personal level. Those facts establish the mortar for the bricks. The goal is to keep history alive."

◆   ◆   ◆

"I love helping others learn to do genealogy. Seeing how to do research and finding their ancestors is so wonderful; I also enjoy each of their successes with things like learning how to organize or record their family history."

III. Love Puzzles and Challenges

Eighteen (21.9 percent) of the responses expressed the love of research, challenges, and puzzles. Many of these respondents also indicated that they enjoyed helping people with their research.

◆   ◆   ◆

"I get a true excitement from the research process. There is something in my nature that loves sleuthing and solving puzzles. I decided that if I was going to 'work,' I wanted to be doing something that I love to do."

◆   ◆   ◆

"The thrill of searching for and finding not only my family history, but actual living, breathing members of my family, whet my appetite for genealogy. I found I have a natural affinity for research. That, plus a life-long love of history, made it a natural choice in a career."

◆   ◆   ◆

"The challenge in researching family lines and finding obscure answers to solve mysteries is a big part of why I do this professionally. Over the years, I found that knowledge of certain areas and the expertise that I had acquired (plus a vast personal library) were of value to those with less experience and resources; so coupled with the lure of 'the hunt,' I began to offer my services."

◆   ◆   ◆

"I enjoy writing. I try to write so that my customers enjoy reading their history. I love genealogy and have a passion for it. In my early school days,

I loved history, reading and literature. When the genealogy 'bug' bit, those early loves became tenacious to a fault. I once spent ten years searching for a single clue—over and over and over I searched, with new angles and new vigor. Finally, after searching through over 5,000 books one long weekend, I found a single paragraph in a single book that led to the discovery of where a brick-wall ancestor had died. I was never so joyful…?"

IV. Career/Job-Transferable Skills

In this category, 13 (15 percent) of the respondents stated that career or job transferable skills were the reason they wanted to become professional genealogists. Those in the fields of law and historical society work, biomedical research, information architect work, instruction in online search, professional writing database development, historical museum work, and music performance found their career work involved many skills that were transferable to genealogical research, and some found that switching to full-time genealogy work was easy and, in some cases, more enjoyable.

◆   ◆   ◆

"My previous career experiences as a content manager, information architect, and instructor in online search skills with my degree in library science and love of problem-solving, with my background in locating, organizing, and navigating online information, the increasing availability of online genealogy data was a significant factor in my decision to undertake a genealogy career."

◆   ◆   ◆

"I am, by education and training, a database developer. Creating tools for genealogists is much more interesting to me than any typical corporate assignments ever were."

◆   ◆   ◆

"My library was a significant local history collection, but nobody has been doing anything with the genealogy section at all. With my genealogy experience and historical training, I became the default point person for the library on local history and genealogy."

◆   ◆   ◆

"Genealogy and law practice are similar in attempting to derive ultimate facts from primary and secondary evidence, through a process of collection, analysis and evaluation of the available evidence, inference and deduction play important roles in both endeavors."

◆   ◆   ◆

"My career was a biomedical researcher. . . switching to full-time paid, genealogy research was easy and more fun than staying in a 9-5 job with a ___boss."

V. Productive Retirement with a Supplemental Income

For ten of the respondents, going professional meant a supplemental income during retirement while doing something that they greatly enjoyed.

◆   ◆   ◆

"My work to that point was so rewarding that I realized I was having too much fun to ever get tired of researching family history, either for myself or others. Retirement was also not far off, so, putting two and two together, I thought by going professional, genealogy will ease the bump in my life that retirement sometimes causes and provide a future of income plus enjoyment."

◆   ◆   ◆

"I am looking to establish a supplemental retirement income involving a field I enjoy and was encouraged to pursue this by the leaders of an NGS research week at Salt Lake City."

◆   ◆   ◆

"I felt my ethnic group has been underserved because of the _____, _____, and language barriers. When the opportunity to retire from the classroom became a reality, I wondered what I would do. I found I could use my teaching skill set to genealogy. I wanted to bring my ethnic group into the mainstream."

VI. Increasing Availability of Resources on the Internet

Only one respondent became a professional genealogist because of the increasing availability of research resources on the Internet. This respondent stated, "With the sources of the Internet, it is now possible to connect with others, share photographs and information as well as access vital records and create online trees. I have become a _____ and a recorder of _____."

Years As A Professional Genealogist And Education

Table 7. Number of Years as a Professional Genealogist

Years	Response Count	Percent (%)
Less than 1	9	10.5
2 to 5	28	32 1
6 to 11	21	24.1
12 to 19	16	18.4
20 to 24	9	10.5
25 to 29	3	3.5
30 to 35	0	0.0
Over 35 yrs	1	1.2
Total	**87**	**100**

N = 87

Respondents were asked how many years they had been professional genealogists (Table 7). The highest percentage of the 87 respondents--32 percent--had been professionals for only two to five years. The second highest percentage of respondents—24 percent—had been professionals from six to eleven years.

Number of Years as a Professional Genealogist and Education

Table 8, a cross-tabulated composite, displays the number of years as a professional genealogist and education by professional certificates, level of education, continuing education, and genealogy educational certificates.

Professional Certificates and Honorary Credentials

Five of the CGs had twelve to nineteen years of experience as professional genealogists; two had two to five years as professional genealogists; and two more had six to eleven years of experience as professional genealogists. Four respondents held AG certification--two with six to eleven years and two with 12 to 19 years of professional experience. Four members held honorary credentials: one Fellow of the American Society of Genealogists (FASG), one Fellow of the Utah Genealogical Society (FUGA), one Fellow of the Genealogical Society of Pennsylvania (FGSP), and one Fellow of the Society of Antiquaries of Scotland (FSA Scotland).

Level of Education

The level of education among the sample was not surprising, since this was a highly educated sample of people. With the exception of five respondents, all had a college education, with 29 holding master's degrees. In addition, two had Ph.D's; one had an Ed.D.; one had a J.D.; and one had a J.D.,L.L.M.

Table 8. Number of Years as a Professional Genealogist and Education

	Number of years of experience as professional genealogist								
Professional Certificate	Less than 1	2-5	6-11	12-19	20-24	25-29	30-35	More than 35 years	Total
CG	0	2	2	5	1	1	0	0	11
CGL	0	0	0	0	0	0	0	0	0
AG	0	0	2	2	0	0	0	0	4
Honorary	0	0	1	2	0	1	0	0	4
None	8	26	18	9	8	2	3	1	75
Total	8	28	23	18	9	4	3	1	94
Level of Education									
High School	0	3	0	0	1	1	0	0	5
Some College	3	5	3	1	1	1	0	0	14
Bachelor's Degree	2	7	8	2	2	0	1	0	22

Number of years of experience as professional genealogist								
Master's Degree	1	9	7	7	3	0	2	0	29
Graduate Studies	2	4	2	4	1	1	0	1	15
Ph.D., Ed.D.	0	0	1	2	0	0	0	0	3
JD	0	0	0	0	1	0	0	0	1
JD, LLM	1	0	0	0	0	0	0	0	1
Total	9	28	21	16	9	3	3	1	90

Continuing Education

Skillbuilding	2	13	14	15	5	2	2	1	54
IGHR	3	6	3	5	2	0	1	0	20
NIGR	3	5	3	6	2	0	0	0	19
BA genealogy at Akamai	0	0	0	0	0	0	0	0	0
BA HGC	0	0	0	0	0	0	0	0	0
Monterrey Penn Com Collage	0	1	0	0	0	0	0	0	1
NGS Home Study	3	11	7	5	1	0	0	1	28
Boston University Certificate	0	0	0	0	0	0	0	0	0
RIGGS Alliance	0	0		1	0	0	0	0	1
None	5	9	6	3	3	2	1	0	29
Total	16	45	33	35	13	4	4	2	152

Genealogy Educational Certificates

The Professional Learning Centre, National Institute for Genealogical Studies, University of Toronto	0	1	0	0	0	0	0	0	1
BYU Certificate in Family History	2	0	2	2	0	0	0	0	6
Heritage Genealogical College Certificate in Genealogy/History	0	0	0	0	0	0	0	0	0
Monterey Peninsula Community College Certificate in Family Research Studies: Genealogy	0	1	0	0	0	0	0	0	1
University of Washington at Seattle Certificate in Genealogy and Family History	0	0	1	0	0	0	0	0	1
No Certificate	6	23	13	10	9	2	2	0	66
Total	8	25	16	12	9	2	2	0	74

Continuing Education

A priority commitment of the NGS was the development of educational programs in genealogy. Initially prompted by the early development of the FASG with its mission of educational development, the BCG's recertification every five years, and the co-sponsorship of IGHR, a week-long Premier Residential seminar was initiated.

The annual national conferences and the co-sponsorship of IGHR reflect the interest of the sponsors and the need for genealogy professionals to participate in continuing education through seminars, institutes, college programs, and local conferences and classes.

In consideration of the high level of education of this sample of respondents and their continuing education, we turn to Houle's conclusions from his studies about adults who are involved in continuing education: "… the most universally important factor is schooling. The higher the formal education of the adult, the more likely it is that he will take part in continuing education. The amount of schooling is, in fact, so significant that it underlies or reinforces many of the other determinants."[69]

The composite Table 8 displays the various institutes, seminars, and programs that are well-known among professional genealogists. Respondents, who were to select all that applied, had participated in a total of 152 seminars or institutes. The Skillbuilding Seminars sponsored by the NGS were especially popular, with 54 respondents attending them .The NGS Home Study Course and the Residential IGHR at Samford University were also popular, with 53 sessions attended. Only 29 respondents had not participated in any of the seminars listed. However, we did not ask about local seminars and continuing education activities in which these genealogists may have participated. (Percentages for the tables in the composite Table 8 are in the Appendices.)

Dates of Attendance at Named Seminars

Respondents were also asked to give the dates of their attendance at the named continuing education sessions. Many of the respondents just indicated number of seminars attended by specific type. Table 10 displays the number of sessions attended over the decades. While this table is not a true picture because of the many non-usable responses, it was considered useful to consider the session attendance over decades. Table 10 does point up some interesting attendance patterns. Although the additional responses without dates could not be used, I listed them in the small chart below.

As can be seen in Table 10, the skillbuilder sessions have by far been the most attended over the three decades by the respondents, with 157 sessions attended. They started to gain popularity in the 1980s.

Next in popularity were the sessions of the IGHR at Samford University, with 53 sessions attended. Next in popularity was the NGS Home Study Course, with 24 courses completed.

While the majority of the professional genealogists in the sample had been professional genealogists for only two to eleven years, Table 9 indicates that 15 respondents had professional certification as CGs or AGs. One member had both CG and AG certification. In addition, Table 9 indicates the increase in respondents' certifications from the year 2000.

Table 9. Professional Certification by Year of First Certification.

Year	CG	CGL	AG	
1981	X			**1**
1993	X			**1**
1997			X	1
1998			X	1
2000	XXX		X	4
2001	X			1
2002				0
2003	X		X	2
2004				0
2005	X			2
2006				0
2007	X			1
2008	0			0
2009	X			1
Total	**11**	**0**	**4**	**15**

N =15   No certification = 75

Table 10. Continuing Education by No. of Sessions Attended over Decades

Type of Continuing Education	Resp.	1970	1980	1990	2000	Total
Skill builder	54	0	16	32	109	157
IGHR	20	3	0	10	40	53
NIGR	19	0	0	6	9	15
BA Akamai Courses	0	0	0	0	0	0
BA HGC Courses	0	0	0	0	0	0
Mont. Comm. College	1	0	0	0	0	0
NGS Home Study	28	0	3	9	12	24
Boston Univ. Courses	0	0	0	0	0	0
Riggs Alliance	1	0	0	0	5	5
NONE ATTENDED	--	-	--	--	--	29
TOTAL	152	3	19	57	175	254

Additional Responses (Did not indicate specific years)

Type of Education.	
Skillbuilders	4, 13, 3-5 yrs, 20, Do not remember, twenty, about 15 years, three, 30+ 3 4, Salt Lake Inst. 6, one, 10, 1 or 2
IGHR	1, one
NIGR	I, one, 3, 1
BA Akamai Courses	0
BA HGC Courses	0
Mont. Comm. College	2 years
NGS Home Study	1, started-bored, two, 2, 2, a long time ago.
Boston Univ. Courses	0
Riggs Alliance	0
Total	----

The chart above displays the responses that I could not place in the table, since only the number of sessions was given, but no dates were provided.

Genealogy Educational Certificates

As can be noted in Table 8, the most popular Genealogy Education Certificate was the Certificate in Family History, with six graduates. The other certificate courses had one or no enrollment from the respondents. Sixty-six respondents did not attend any of the Genealogy General Education Certificate programs.

Professional Tasks Carried Out And Time Spent As Professional Genealogists

The respondents were asked to identify the type of professional tasks they performed. They could select all that applied. As Table 11 indicates, 66 (79.5 percent) of the 83 respondents who answered the question did contract work for clients; 41 (49.4 percent) taught genealogy courses; and 40 (48.2 percent) wrote about genealogy and delivered presentations at seminars and conferences. Twenty-two respondents (26.5 percent) had written books. Over the previous decade, the respondents had produced a total of 56 books, in addition to six cemetery books and 22 client books.

Table 11. Professional Tasks of Professional Genealogists

Type of Work	Responses	Percent (%)
Own a bookstore genealogy supply or publishing business	6	7.3
Contract work for clients	66	79.5
Write about genealogy	40	48.2
Coordinate conferences and events	17	20.5
Deliver presentations at seminars and conferences	40	48.2
Teach genealogy courses	41	49.4
Write books	22	26. 5
Total books written	84 (six cemetery books, 22client books, and 56 others)	

$N = 83$

Write about Genealogy

Respondents were asked to select the type of publications for which they wrote. They were to select all that applied. Table 12 indicates that 32 (82.1percent) of the respondents wrote for society and organization publications without pay.

Table 12. Write about Genealogy

Type of Publications	Responses	Percent (%)
For-pay commercial publications and services	15	38.5
Peer-reviewed research publications	14	35.9
Society and organization publications, without pay	32	82.1

$N = 38$

Teach Genealogy

If respondents taught genealogy courses, they were asked to indicate where they taught.

Table 13. Teach Genealogy Courses

Type of Course	Response	Percent (%)
Local conferences	30	69.8
National conferences	11	25.6
Continuing education classes	15	34.9
One- or two-day scheduled seminars	29	67.4
Annual residential classes	2	4.7
Univ. college genealogy degree program	0	0.0
Genealogy certificate program	1	2.3
All of the above	0	0.0
Total	**43**	

$N = 43$

Table 13 indicates that 69.8 percent of the 43 respondents taught at local conferences and 67.4 percent taught at one- or two-day scheduled seminars

Respondents who wrote books (question 12) were asked to select whether they wrote for commercial publishers or for self-publishing clients or genealogists. Of the 26 respondents who answered that question, 78 percent of the respondents indicated they were self-published by clients or genealogists.

Type of Work Organization

Respondents were asked to indicate the type of work organization in which they were involved. As Table 14 indicates, 71 (86.6 percent) of the 83 respondents were self-employed genealogists. Thirteen answered "other" and indicated a variety of other types of work situations (e.g., coordinator of an annual three-day conference for thirteen years, publisher of a newsletter, officer of a state genealogical society, and genealogist for a lineage society).

Table 14. Type of Work Organization

Organization	Response	Percent (%)
Self-employed	71	86.6
Gen. research or services org.	4	4.9
Librarian, curator, archivist	6	7.3
Gen employment in a non-gen. org.	2	2.4
Teacher in educational institution	2	2.4
Inst./Prof. in genealogy in higher education	0	0.0
Admin/teacher in online, virtual environment	1	1.2
Other	13	15.7
Assist individuals for memberships in SAR, DAR,CDXVIC, MAGNA CHARTA, AND OTHERS	1	

Own genealogist firm	1
Officer of state gen. society	1
Coordinate an annual three-day conference for thirteen yrs.	1
Publisher of newsletter	1
Tribal genealogist and research asst. for individual CG	1
Genealogist for lineage societies	1
Full-time another profession	1
Assist an experienced professional genealogist with research for pay and I learn	1
Work online for genealogy publisher	1
Outside of professional genealogy; librarian and professor of higher education	1
Volunteer New England Historical Gen Society, county, Hist. Soc. and librarian at local family hist. center	1

N = 83

Table 15. National Conferences Attended over the Past Five Years

Number of National Conferences Attended Past 5 Years	Responses	Percent (%)
1 TO 2	25	28.7
3 TO 5	29	33.3
6 TO 10	9	10.3
11 TO 15	2	2.3
16 TO 20	0	0.0
20 OR MORE	0	0.0
NONE	22	25.3

$N = 87$

National Conference Attendance

National conferences draw approximately 1,600 genealogists annually, with peak years drawing over 2,000. Approximately 200 to 250 presenters are scheduled.[70] This is the arena where professionals learn, network, and hold meetings. The professional genealogists of this sample were indeed attendees of national conferences, such as the NGS and the FGS, where the Skillbuilder sessions sponsored by the BCG are taught. The two national conferences appeal to different groups: the national NGS conferences appeal to individuals, and the FGS conferences appeal to local societies as members.[71]

Table 15 displays the attendance of 87 respondents at national conferences over the past five years. Twenty-nine professionals (33.3 percent) indicated that they had attended three to five national conferences over the past five years; 25 respondents (28.7 percent) indicated they had attended one to two conferences; and nine respondents (0.3 percent) stated that they had attended six to ten national conferences over the past five years. Two (2.3 percent) of the respondents had attended eleven to fifteen national conferences. However, 25.3 percent of the respondents indicated they had not attended any national conferences over the past five years.

Table 16. Time Spent in Genealogy Work per Week

Hours per week	Response	Percent (%)
5 to 10 hours	12	13.8
11 to 20 hours	22	25.3
21 to 35 hours	22	25.3
36 to 40 hours	16	18.4
41 to 46 hours	4	4.6
47 to 55 hours	11	12.6

$N = 87$

Table 16 indicates the amount of time the respondent professionals spent in genealogy work per week. This includes all activities related to genealogy. Twenty-two (25.3 percent) of the 87 respondents spend from eleven to twenty hours per week on genealogical work, and 22 (25.3 percent) spend from 21 to 35 hours. Eleven respondents (12 percent) of the 87 spend 47 to 55 hours on genealogy work per week.

In response to the last question, which asked for additional information the respondent wanted to share, one respondent claimed to work an average of 70 to 80 hours per week on genealogy.

Years in the Profession and Time Spent in Genealogy

Table 17 displays the number of years respondents had been professional genealogists and the amount of time they spent on genealogical activities.

Table 17. Years in the Profession and Time Spent in Genealogy

Time spent in genealogy	Less than One Year	Two to Five Years	Six to Eleven Years	Twelve to Nineteen Years	Twenty to Twenty-four Years	Twenty-five to Twenty-nine Years	Over Thirty-five Years	Total Years
5 to 10 hours	1	7	2	--	1	1	--	**12**
11 to 20 hours	1	5	7	4	2	1	--	**20**
21 to 35 hours	3	7	7	4	--	1	--	**22**
36 to 40 hours	3	4	1	5	2	--	1	**16**
41 to 46 hours	--	2	1	1	--	--	--	**4**
47 to 55 hours	--	4	2	2	3	--	--	**11**
Total hours	**8**	**29**	**20**	**16**	**8**	**3**	**1**	**85**

N = 85

The largest number of people—22—spent from 21 to 35 hours on genealogical activity. These respondents were in all categories except 20 to 24 and over 35 years as professionals. The 20 persons who spent eleven to 20 hours were in all categories of professionals, as indicated by number of years in the profession. Of the eleven respondents who spent 47 to 55 hours on genealogical activities, four had been professionals from two to five years, two from six to eleven years, two from 12 to 19 years, and three from 20 to 24 years.

Conclusions And Model Of Why I Became A Professional Genealogist

This study focused on why people became interested and studied genealogy, and why they decided to become professional genealogists. The findings strongly emphasize the strength of kinfolk in maintaining their roles as keepers of the family records, the family traditions, the teaching about the family to the growing generations, and, most importantly, stimulating these respondents toward the study of genealogy and becoming professionals. A major conclusion reached in this study is that the momentum toward the increasing professionalism in genealogy is fostered by strong leadership at the national level, which flows through all levels and integrated areas of genealogy.

Model of Why I Became a Professional Genealogist

The major conclusion reached in this study was that the interest in becoming a professional genealogist is stimulated by strong leadership at the national level, which is driven by continual reinforcement of high standards and by the emphasis on education and continuing education, which flows across all levels. Such emphasis was evident in the respondents' responses in their written paragraphs explaining why they wanted to be professionals, as they stated that they wanted to know and learn more; in their present level of education; in their attendance at national association conferences; in their participation in educational seminars and training programs; in their earning of certification status; in their writing, teaching, and making presentations to groups; and in the hours of work they spend per week on their genealogical activities.

After completing the analyses of the survey questions and noting the strong leadership results evident in the responses of the professionals regarding their reasons for becoming professionals and their excitement about becoming the type of genealogist who really knows how to do genealogy, I returned to the data in the published literature to analyze the development of the national professional groups. I then developed a model to depict the Professionalization of the Genealogist, which appears on the next page. This model is based on three components: <u>Strong Leadership at the National Level</u>, driven by <u>High</u> <u>Standards in Research and Writing</u>, and <u>Education and Continuing Education</u>.

This leadership model is an emergent model that goes beyond the Senge model of the "learning organization," which maintains that leaders of the 21st century are designers, stewards, and teachers.[76] It is a leadership model of multimodal systems on an international level. Its implementation should be studied further, as it is a leadership model for multiorganizations in a multimodal interorganizational setting.

<u>Began to Study Genealogy</u>

Kinfolk inspired continue to learn
Curious Just wanted to know
Business Career Job Related School
College Church Assignment Project
Religion
Fascination with history
Family help no information
Friends helping friends

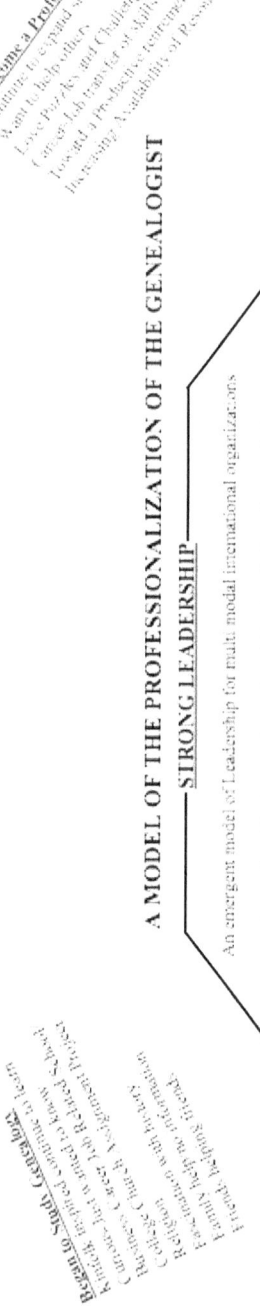

<u>To Become a Professional</u>

Continue to expand skills and Learn More
Want to help others
Love Puzzles and Challenges
Career Job transfer of skills
Toward a Productive retirement
Increasing Availability of Resources

A MODEL OF THE PROFESSIONALIZATION OF THE GENEALOGIST

STRONG LEADERSHIP

An emergent model of Leadership for multi modal international organizations

(more than "Designers, Stewards and Teachers" (Peter Senge,(1990)

HIGH STANDARDS IN RESEARCH AND WRITING

•1996– Board for Certification of Genealogists Skill builders for Certification At National Conferences

BCG Standards Manual

-Certification Standards

-Standard of Proof

-Certification Examinations Re-certification every 5 years CG and CGL

1903 National Genealogical Society NGS—Washington D.C.
"to educate the genealogical community"
Lectures, conferences-courses
Saturday lectures for twenty years
2001 online-lectures (Wilcox, 2003,251)
2003 Audio-tape conferences (Wilcox, 2003, 251)
1912 NGS Quarterly
1981 Conference in the States- a series of annual Conferences-educational programs (1600-2000 persons, 200—250 presenters)

•1940– American Society of Genealogists– 50 elected Fellows Committed to upgrade standards in genealogy
1979– Association of Professional Genealogists "To create awareness and interest in genealogy"
24 chapters (Moody 2007,p.254)
online forum for networking and learning
Directory of Members online
APG Quarterly

Family History Library of Salt Lake City

EDUCATION AND CONTINUING EDUCATION

•1950– National Institute for Genealogical Research at the National Archives

•1964 Samford University
IGHR – Institute for Genealogy and Historical Research week long residential program taught by top scholars in the fields

1981 NGS –National Genealogical Society Home Study Course

[illegible]

Recommendations For Further Research

1. A fruitful and practical area for further research would be to interview professional genealogists and analyze their concerns in their professional roles. The present study indicated that 66 (79.5 percent) of the 83 respondents did contract work for clients; 40 (48.2 percent) delivered presentations at seminars and conferences; and 41 (49.4 percent) taught genealogy courses. A needs assessment of professional genealogists would help determine their concerns in these tasks and could be effectively used to develop seminars, courses, and workshops.

2. More research with different groups is needed to determine why they decided to study genealogy. Some of these respondents should be interviewed for more information regarding their decision to become certified genealogists.

3. An important aspect of the present study was the vibrant, energetic, functional leadership that flows from the national groups. Within the responses of the sample of professional genealogists, the leadership inherent in the national genealogy groups inspires and directs professional genealogists in an extraordinary manner as it flows into individual goals and activities, continuing education, and the professionals' daily tasks.

This effective leadership model of the genealogy profession is one to be studied as an example of a 21st century model of leadership in multimodal international organization flows. The model of leadership in organizations that replaced the male-oriented models of the Industrial Era was developed by Peter Senge of MIT in the 1990s and is described in his book *The Fifth Discipline,* as he developed a model of leaders as designers, stewards, and teachers for organizations of the 21st century.[77] His model is left behind as a one-organizational view with the power of effective leadership, as implemented in the field of genealogy.

The emergent genealogical leadership model depicted on the preceding page should be researched and brought forward as a prototype of a model of leadership for the multimodal, multiorganizational, and multinational leadership of the 21st century.

Endnotes

1. Sharon Tate Moody, "The State of the Association. A Year-End Status Report," *Association of Professional Genealogists Quarterly*, 12, 4 (2007), 153-154.
2. Margot Hornblower, "Roots Mania," *Time,* April 19, Vol 153, 15, 2.
3. Alex Haley, *Roots* (New York: Garden City, 1976).
    See Elizabeth Shown Mills and Gary P. Mills, "The Genealogist's Assessment of Alex Haley's *Roots.*"
    National Genealogical Society Quarterly, 72, 1, 1984, 35-49. The authors provide the evidence that this work is fictionalized. They discuss the deleterious effects on black history and the field of genealogy. They also maintain that this work raises the issue of professional standards, with which genealogists were currently grappling as they were striving to raise the image of the profession.
4. David Popenoe, *Life Without Father* (Cambridge: Harvard University Press, 1996), 139-164.
    Dr. Popenoe draws out the research evidence of fatherlessness in our American society and why fathers matter.
    Another study and book by David Blankenhorn, *Fatherless America* (New York: Harper, 1995), draws from research on the lack of fathers in the homes, providing evidence that this is an urgent social problem in American society. He reflects historically on the advent of industrialization and the father leaving the home for paid work, which led to the loss of father power of the family and in the family.
5. Donn Devine, "Defining Professionalism," in *Professional Genealogy: A Manual for Researchers, Writers, Editors, Lecturers, and Librarians,* ed. Elizabeth Shown Mills (Baltimore: Genealogical Publishing Co., 2001),12.
6. Ibid., 12.
7. Ibid., 5. Descriptions for each point are author's paraphrased summaries.
8. Robert M. Taylor, Jr., and Ralph J. Crandall, "Historians and Genealogists: An Emerging Community of Interest," in *Generations and Change: Genealogical Perspectives in Social History*, eds. Robert M. Taylor, Jr., and Ralph J. Crandall (Macon: Mercer University Press, 1986), 5.
9. Ibid., 4, 5.
10. Ibid., 6.
11. Ibid., 12.

12. Lewis Paul Todd and Merle Curti, *Rise of the American Nation* (New York: Harcourt, Brace and World, Inc., 1961), 429.

13. Andrew Cherlin, *Public and Private Families* (Boston: McGraw Hill, 1999), 52-53.

14. Taylor and Crandall, "Historians and Genealogists," 8.

15. Cherlin, *Public and Private Families*, 53; U. S. Bureau of Census, 1975.

16. Taylor and Crandall, "Historians and Genealogists," 9.

17. Ibid., 9.

18. Ibid., 1l.

19. Ibid., 14.

20. Steven Pinker, "Strangled by Roots," *New Republic,* August 6, 2007, 32-35. http://pinker, wjh.harvard.edu. (accessed Jan. 25, 2000).

21. John Seabrook, "The Tree of Me," *The New Yorker,* Mar. 26, 2001, Vol. 23, 1.

22. Marc Peyser and Claudia Kolb, "Roots Network," *Newsweek*, February 24, 1997, 33.

23. Cyndi's List of Genealogy Sites on the Internet, 1996-2009, Historical Timeline, http://cindislist.com/faq/timeline.htm. (Accessed February 1, 2009).

24. Kevin Steel, "All Roads Lead to Salt Lake City," *Alberta Report*, Vol, 24, 43 pages, October 6, 1997. P1. http://webebscohost.com/ehost/detail (Accessed Mar. 4, 2009).

25. Margot Hornblower, "Roots Mania," *Time*, Vol. 153, 15, April 19, 1999, 56.

26. Angela J. Krum, "Tracking your Roots Online," *Parenting, Family Reporter/News Trends Voices, Views,* September 1, 1999. http:// elibrary. Big chalk.com /libweb/curriculum/do/document? set=to. (Accessed March 5, 2009).

27. Michael Saul, "Ellis Isle Web Site Flooded With Genealogy Inquiries," *New York Daily News,* May 13, 2001, 34.

28. "Look Homeward, Boomer: A Younger Generation Takes an Interest in Genealogy," *The Seattle Times*, August 4, 1996, pL1. Infotrac Newspapers, http://find.galegroup.com/itx. (Accessed March 5, 2009).

29. Jennifer Fulkerson, "Climbing the Family Tree," *American Demographics,* December 1995, 42-51.

30. Generations Network, "Survey Reveals Americans' Surprising Lack of Family Knowledge," December 6, 200? Source: Omnibus Survey, Market Tools, and Feb. 2007). http://tgn.media room.com/index.php? s 438 item'115. (Accessed March 13, 2009).

31. Ronald Bishop, "The Essential Force of the Clan: Developing a Collecting-Inspired Ideology of Genealogy Through Textual Analysis,"

Journal of Popular Culture, 38, no. 6 (2005): 990-1010. ebscohost.com/ehost/results? (Accessed March 14, 2009).

32. Jean Baudrillard, *The System of Objects*, (London: Verso, 1996) cited in Bishop, p. 991, "The Essential Force of the Clan: "Developing a Collecting-Inspired Ideology of Genealogy Through Textual Analysis." *The Journal of Popular Culture,* Vol. 38, No. 6, 2005, 992.

33. Bishop, "The Essential Force of the Clan," 1007.

34. Barb Kindaris, "E-Reference Ratings," *Library Journal* 134, no. 5 (2009): 126-127. Provided to e-list of APG members by Christine Crawford Oppenheimer.

Nine software programs for genealogy are described and ranked as to scope, writing, design, bells and whistles, ease of use, linking, and value. Available online at Ancestry, Footnote.com, Genealogy Bank, and others. http://www.libraryjournal.com/article/CA6643144htm

35. Doug Erickson, "Who Lurks in your Past? Was the Duke of Wellington One of your Ancestors? DNA Testing, by Private Companies May be Able to Help you Fill Out your Family Tree." *Wisconsin State Journal*, Dec. 9, 2007, PA1. http://findgalegroup,com/itx/retrieve.doc accessed 3/5/09.

36. Zina Moukheiber, "Genes for Sale," July 27, 1998, 1-3 http://web.ebscohost.com//ehost. (Accessed March 4, 2009).

37. John Seabrook, "The Tree of Me, DNA Testing is Revolutionizing the Field of Genealogy." *The New Yorker*, March 26, 2001, 58.

38. Peter Senge, *The Fifth Discipline*: *The Art and Practice of the Learning Organization* (New York: Doubleday, 1990).

39. Elizabeth Shown Mills, "Genealogy in the Information Age: History's New Frontier?" *National Genealogical Society Quarterly* 91, (2003), 265.

40. Shirley Langdon Wilcox, "The National Genealogical Society: A Look at Its First One Hundred Years*," The National Genealogical Society Quarterly* 91 (2003), 246.

41. Donn Devine e-mail to author, May 23, 2009.

42. Ibid, June 4, 2009.

43. Wilcox, "The National Genealogical Society," 251, 252, 253, 254.

See Elizabeth Shown Mills, "Genealogy in the Information Age." Ms. Mills points out, "Progress had been made as: *The NGS Quarterly*--which cracked a corner of an academic barricade seventeen years ago with university-based editors and editorial offices has--earned some acceptance among historians.. Relevant items from the NGS Quarterly were included in the calendars of Record Scholarship by major history journals, such as The *Journal of American History and Journal of Southern History.*"

44. Jennifer Taylor, Technical Archivist, Samford University, http://www.

Samford.edu/Schools/IGHR/IGHR- history.html. 1-2 (Accessed May 6, 2009).

45. Ibid.

46. Loretta Evans, "Beyond the Alphabet Soup: Who are Accredited Genealogists?" *Association of Professional Genealogists Quarterly* 17, 4, December 2002, 141.

47. Kay Haviland Freilich, "BCG History," *On Board* 7, no. 1 (2001). http:// www.bcgcertification.org/about bcg/ bchistory.hgtml. (Accessed, June 13, 2009).

48. Lynn McMillion, BCG Executive Director, e-mail to author, April 11, 2009.

Note: The CG examination must be retaken every five years. An individual must pass the certification standards to maintain the CG credential status.

49. William Litchman, "Applying for Certification? It's Worth It." *Association of Professional Genealogists Quarterly*, 11, 3 Sept. 1996, 78-79.
    Also, see Thomas W. Jones "Certification--What does it Really Mean?" *Association of Professional Genealogists Quarterly*, 14, 5, Dec. 1999, 166-169.

50. Family History Library, http:/Family Search.org Eng/Library/FHL/ Framewet-library.asp? pa frameset-library-asp? PAGE= library-history. asp=library-history.asp_and telephone response to my call on 2/12/2009. Family History Library Public Affairs.

51. Federation of Genealogical Societies, "Linking the Genealogical Community," http:/www.fgs.org. Accessed Feb. 8, 2009.

52. Glade Nelson and supplemented by Alice Eichholz, "A Brief History of the Association of Professional Genealogists," VI, 1, spring, 1991, 24. *Adapted from APG Quarterly*, 1, 4, winter, 1986 14-17 (as prepared by Glade Nelson and supplemented by Alice Eichholz).

53. Sharon Tate Moody, "The State of the Association: A Year-end Status Report," *Association of Professional Genealogists Quarterly*, 12, 4, 2007, 153, 154.

54. Ibid., 153.

55. Kathleen Hinckley, "APG Membership Facts and Figures Reveal Diversity," *Association of Professional Genealogists Quarterly*, 18, 1, 2003, 8.

56. Elizabeth Shown Mills, "Academia vs. Genealogy Prospects for Reconciliation and Progress," *National Genealogical Society Quarterly*, 71, 2, 1983, 99-106.

57. Ibid., 106.

58. The Billingsley Kinship theoretical framework was developed in Dr. Carolyn Earle Billingsley's doctoral dissertation and is contained in her book *Communities of Kinship, Antebellum Families and the Settlement of the Cotton Frontier* (Univ. of Georgia Press, 2004). This work served as

the first step for the field of genealogical studies to be accepted in higher education. It will now move on to define its place in higher education.

59. The Sloan Consortium, "Staying the Course, Online Education in the United States, 2008," http://www.Sloan-c.org/publications/survey/index.asp, accessed 5/27/09.

60. Sharan B. Merriam, *Case Study Research in Education, A Qualitative Approach*, (San Francisco: Jossey Bass Pub, 1988), 47-48.

61. Earl Babbie, *Survey Research Methods*, (Belmont: Wadsworth Pub. Co., 1973), 76-78.

62. Mihaly Csikszentmihalyi and Eugene Rochberg-Halton, *The Meaning of Things: Domestic Symbols and the Self*, (New York: Cambridge University Press, 1981), 248.

63. Ibid., 248-249.

64. Ibid., 249.

65. Herbert J. Klausmeier and William Goodwin, *Learning and Human Abilities*, 2nd ed. (New York: Harper and Row, 1966), 427.

66. Ibid., 426.

67. A.H. Maslow, *The Farther Reaches of Human Nature,* (New York: Viking Press, 1971), 301.

68. Csikszentmihalyi and Rochberg-Halton, 248-249.

69. Cyril Houle, *The Inquiring Mind*, (Madison: Univ. of Wis. Press, 1961).

70. Donn Devine, e-mail to author, May 23, 2009.

71. Ibid.

72. Klausmeier and Goodwin, *Learning and Human Abilities*, 427.

73. Ibid., 426

74. Maslow, The *Farther Reaches of Human Nature*, 301.

75. Ibid.

76. Peter Senge, *The Fifth Discipline.*

77. Ibid.

References

Babbie, Earl. *Survey Research Methods.* (Belmont: Wadsworth Pub Co., 1973).

Baudrillard, Jean. *The System of Objects.* (London: Verso, 1996).

Billingslsey, Carolyn Earle. *Communities of Kinship, Antebellum Families and the Settlement of the Cotton Frontier.* (Univ. of Georgia Press: Athens, 2004).

Bishop, Ronald. "The essential force of the clan: Developing a collecting-inspired idealogy of genealogy through textual analysis." *Journal of Popular Culture*, 38, no. 6 (2005): 990-1010 ebscohost. Com/ehost/results? Accessed March 14, 2009.

Blankenhorn, David. *Fatherless America* (New York: Harper, 1995).

Cherlin, Andrew. *Public and Private Families* (Boston: McGraw Hill, 1999).

Csikszentmihalyi and Eugene Rochbert-Halton. *The Meaning of Things: Domestic Symbols and the Self.* (New York: Cambridge University Press, 1981).

Cyndi's List of Genealogy Sites on the Internet. 1996-2009.
Historical Timeline, http://cindislist.com/faqltimeline.htm. Accessed February 1, 2009.

Devine, Donn. "Defining Professionalism" in *Professional Genealogy: a Manual for Researchers, Writers, Editors, Lecturers, and Librarians*, ed., Elizabeth Shown Mills. (Baltimore: Genealogical Publishing Co., 2001), 5-14.

_____. E-mail to author in response to author's query on current attendance at National Conferences each year. May 23, 2009.

_____. E-mail to author in response to query on overseas honorary credentials. June 4, 2009.

Erickson, Doug. "Who Lurks in Your Past? Was the Duke of Wellington One of Your Ancestors? DNA Testing by Private Companies May be able to Help You Fill Out Your Family Tree." *Wisconsin State Journal,* December 9, 2007, PA1-11 InfotracNewspapers.http //find, gale group.com/itx / retrieve.do? Accessed March 4, 2009.

Evans, Loretta. "Beyond the Alphabet Soup: Who are Accredited Genealogists?" *Association of Professional Genealogists Quarterly 17, 4,* December 2002, 141-141.

Family History Library, Public Affairs. http://Family Search.org Eng/ Library/ FHL/ Framewer-library.asp? pa. Telephone Response call on February 12, 2000.

Federation of Genealogical Societies. "Linking the Genealogical Community," http:// www. fgs.org. Accessed February 8, 2009.

Freilich, Kay Haviland. "BCG History*,"* *On Board*, 7, no. 1, 2001, http:// www.bcgcertification.org/about bcg/ bchistory.hgtml. Accessed June 13, 2009.

Fulkerson, Jennifer. "Climbing the Family Tree," *American Demographics*, December 1995. 42-51.

Generations Network. "Survey Reveals Americans' Surprising Lack of Family Knowledge," December 6, 2007 and February 2006, (Press Release) http://tgn.mediaroom.com/index.php? 438 i&item=1145. Accessed March 13, 2009.

Haley, Alex. *Roots*, (New York: Garden City, 1976).

Hinckley, Kathleen. "APG Membership Facts and Figures Reveal Diversity," *Association of Professional Genealogists Quarterly*, 18,1, 2003, 8.

Hornblower, Margot. "Roots Mania," *Time*, April 19, 1999, 15, 2.

Houle, Cyril. *The Inquiring Mind, a Study of the Adult Learner who Continues to Learn,* (Madison: University of Wisconsin Press, 1961).

Jones, Thomas W. "Certification, What Does it Really Mean?" *Association of Professional Genealogists Quarterly, 14,5*, December 1999, 166-169.

Kindaris, Barb. "E-Reference Ratings,*" Library Journal, 134, 5*, 126-127. http: www.libraryjournal.com/article/CA6643144html Accessed April 10, 2009.

Klausmeier, Herbert J., and William Goodwin. *Learning and Human Abilities*, 2nd ed. (New York: Harper and Row, 1966).

Krum, Angela, "Tracking Your Roots Online," Parenting, Family Reporter/ News, Trends, Voices, Views. September 1, 1999. Http://elibrary, Bigchalk.com/ libweb/curriculum /do/document set=to. Accessed March 5, 2009 .

Litchman, William. "Applying for Certification, It's Worth It." *Association of Professional Genealogists Quarterly*, 11, 3, September 1996, 78-79.

Maslow, A.H. *The Farther Reaches of Human Nature* (New York: Viking Press, 1971).

McMillion, Lynn C., e-mail to author, LaWanna Lease Blount, Ph.D., April 11, 2009.

Merriam, Sharan B. *Case Study Research in Education, A Qualitative Approach*, (San Francisco: Jossey Bass Pub., 1988.)

Mills, Elizabeth Shown, ed. *Professional Genealogy: A Manual for Researchers, Writers, Editors, Lecturers, and Librarians* (Baltimore: Genealogical Pub. Co., 2001).

_____. "Genealogy in the Information Age: History's New Frontier?" *National Genealogical Society Quarterly* 91, 12, 2003, 260-277.

Mills, Elizabeth Shown and Gary P. Mills, "The Genealogists Assessment of Alex Haley's *Roots*," *National Genealogical Society Quarterly*, 72, 1, 1984, 35-49.

Moody , Sharon Tate. "The State of the Association: A Year-end Status Report," *Association of Professional Genealogists Quarterly*, 12, 4, 153-154.

Moukheiber, Zina. "Genes For Sale," July 27, 1998, 1-3. Http://web.ebscohot.com//ehost. Accessed March 4, 2009.

Nelson, Glade and Alice Eichholz. "A Brief History of the Association of Professional Genealogists," VI, 1 Spring, 1991, 24, adapted from APG Quarterly 1, 4, winter, 1986, 14-17. (as prepared by Glade Nelson and supplemented by Alice Eichholz.).

Peyser, Marc and Claudia Kolb. "Roots Network," *Newsweek*, February 24, 1997, 33

Pinker, Steven. "Strangled by Roots," *The New Republic*, August 6, 2007, 32-35. http//: pinker, wjh.harvard.edu/articles/media/ reprint, unpaged 8 pages. Accessed January 25, 2008.

Popenoe, David. *Life Without Father* (Cambridge: Harvard University Press, 1996).

Saul, Michael. "Ellis Isle Website Flooded With Genealogy Inquiries," *New York Daily News*, May 13, 2001, 34.
Online archives, www.nydailynews.come/archives/news/2001/05/13/=05-13ellis-isle Web-site-flooded: (Interlibrary loan, 5/13/2009.)

Seabrook, John. "The Tree of Me, DNA Testing is Revolutionizing the Field of Genealogy*," The New Yorker*, March 26, 2001, 58.

Senge, Peter. *The Fifth Discipline, The Art and Practice of The Learning Organization,* (New York: Doubleday, 1990) .

Sloan Consortium. "Staying the Course, Online Education in the United States, 2008," http: // www.Sloan-c.org/publications/survey/index.asp. Accessed May 27, 2009.

Steel Kevin. "All Roads Lead to Salt Lake City," *Alberta Report/ Newsmagazine*, vol. 24, 43, Oct., 6, 1997, 1-3 . http://webebscohost.com/ehost. Accessed March 4, 2009.

Taylor, Jennifer. Samford University Library, IGHR, History , http://www. Samford.edu/schools/IGHr/IGHr-history 1-2 Accessed May 6, 2009.

Taylor, Robert M., Jr., and Ralph J. Crandall, eds. *Generations and Change:*

Genealogical Perspectives in Social History, (Macon: Mercer University Press, 1986).

Taylor, Robert M, Jr., and Ralph J. Crandall, "Historians and Genealogists: An Emerging Community of Interest," in *Generations and Change: Genealogical Perspectives in Social History*, eds. Robert M. Taylor, Jr., and Ralph J. Crandall, (Macon, Mercer University Press, 1986), Chapter 1, 4-27.

The Seattle Times. "Look Homeward, Boomer: A Younger Generation Takes An Interest in Genealogy," August 4, 1996, PL.1.
Infotrac Newspapers, http:// find.galegroup.com/itx. Accessed March 5, 2009.

Todd, Lewis Paul and Merle Curti, *Rise of the American Nation* (New York: Harcourt Brace and World, Inc., 1961).

Wilcox, Shirley Langdon, "The National Genealogical Society: A Look at Its First One Hundred Years," *The National Genealogical Society Quarterly* 91, 12, 2003, 245-259.

APPENDICES

Number of years of experience as professional genealogist

Professional Certificate	Less than 1	2-5	6-11	12-19	20-24	25-29	30-35	More than 35 years	Total	Percentages
CG	0	2	2	5	1	1	0	0	11	11.70%
CGL	0	0	0	0	0	0	0	0	0	
AG	0	0	2	2	0	0	0	0	4	4.26%
Honorary	0	0	1	2	0	1	0	0	4	4.26%
None	8	26	18	9	8	2	3	1	75	79.79%
Total percentages	8	28	23	18	9	4	3	1	94	100.00%
	8.51%	29.79%	24.47%	19.15%	9.57%	4.26%	3.19	1.06%	100.00%	

Level of Education	Less than 1	2-5	6-11	12-19	20-24	25-29	30-35	More than 35 years	Total	Percentages
High School	0	3	0	0	1	1	0	0	5	5.56%
Some College	3	5	3	1	1	1	0	0	14	15.56%
Bachelor's Degree	2	7	8	2	2	0	1	0	22	24.44%
Master's Degree	1	9	7	7	3	0	2	0	29	32.22%
Graduate Studies	2	4	2	4	1	1	0	1	15	16.67%
PhD EdD	0	0	1	2	0	0	0	0	3	3.33%
JD	0	0	0	0	1	0	0	0	1	1.11%
JD LLM	1	0	0	0	0	0	0	0	1	1.11%
Total Percentages	9	28	21	16	9	3	3	1	90	100.00%
	10.00%	31.11%	23.33%	17.78%	10.00%	3.33%	3.33%	1.11%	100.00%	

Table 8 with Percentages pages 60-61.

Continuing Education | **Number of years of experience as professional genealogist**

Continuing Education	Number of years of experience as professional genealogist									
Skillbuilders	2	13	14	15	5	2	2	1	54	35.53%
IGHR	3	6	3	5	2	0	1	0	20	13.16%
NIGR	3	5	3	6	2	0	0	0	19	12.50%
BA genealogy at Akamai	0	0	0	0	0	0	0	0	0	--
BA HGC	0	0	0	0	0	0	0	0	0	--
Monterey Penn Com Collage	0	1	0	0	0	0	0	0	1	0.66%
NGS Home Study	3	11	7	5	1	0	0	1	28	18.42%
Boston University Certificate	0	0	0	0	0	0	0	0	0	--
RIGGS Alliance	0	0	1	1	0	0	0	0	1	0.66%
None	5	9	6	3	3	2	1	0	29	19.08%
Total	16	45	33	35	13	4	4	2	152	100.00%
	10.53%	29.61%	21.71%	23.03%	8.55%	2.63%	2.63%	1.32%	100.00%	

Genealogy Educational Certificates | **Number of years of experience as professional genealogist**

Genealogy Educational Certificates	Number of years of experience as professional genealogist									
The Professional Learning Centre, National Institute for Genealogical Studies, University of Toronto	0	1	0	0	0	0	0	0	1	1.35%
BYU Certificate in Family History	2	0	2	2	0	0	0	0	6	8.11%
Heritage Genealogical College Certificate in Genealogy/History	0	0	0	0	0	0	0	0	0	--
Monterey Peninsula Community College Certificate in Family Research Studies: Genealogy	0	1	0	0	0	0	0	0	1	1.35%
University of Washington at Seattle Certificate in Genealogy and Family History	0	0	1	0	0	0	0	0	1	1.35%
No Certificate	6	23	13	10	9	2	2	0	66	89.19%
Total	8	25	16	12	9	2	2	0	74	100.00%
	10.81%	33.78%	21.62%	16.22%	12.16%	2.70%	2.70%	0.00%	100.00%	

Table 8 with Percentages, pages 60 and 61

Interest in Genealogy and Becoming a Professional Genealogist

As stated in the introductory letter, you have been selected to participate in this study. If you have any questions, please contact me directly through my email included in the cover letter.

To progress through this survey, please use the navigation buttons located on the bottom of the pages:

- **Continue** to the next page of the survey by clicking the *Continue to the Next Page* link.
- **Go back** to the previous page in the survey by clicking on the *Previous Page* link. This will allow you to move back in the survey to look over the previous answers.
- **Finish** the survey, by clicking the *Submit the Survey* link on the Thank You page.

Your participation in the survey will provide insightful information.

Thanks again for your effort and response!

Interest in Genealogy and Becoming a Professional Genealogist

Please mark your response by checking the appropriate answer. Some may ask for more than one answer but will clearly state this in the question instructions.

1. The number of years that you have been involved in genealogy:

○ Less than one
○ 1 to 5
○ 6 to 9
○ 7 to 10
○ 11 to 15
○ 16 to 20
○ 21 to 26
○ 27 to 35
○ more than 35 years

2. Age:

○ Under 30
○ 31 to 40
○ 41 to 50
○ 51 to 60
○ 61 to 70
○ 71 to 80
○ over 80

3. Why I became interested in genealogy. Mark an X on the closest main reason:

○ A close relative had many antiques, artifacts, and old papers that fascinated me

○ My parents were divorced and I did not know one of them, or any of the family

○ Some one I knew was tracing their family tree and found it fascinating

○ A close relative was tracing family lineage and I saw how interesting it was

○ My spouse was tracing his/her family lineage

○ A teacher, professor inspired me by telling the class stories about ancestors

○ In school we were assigned a project / after school youth activity in genealogy

○ A parent died when I was very young and I wanted to know more about my ancestors

○ I was adopted and wanted to find my birth parents and kinfolk

○ We had moved so much I did not know my kin

○ I was fascinated with the family databases on the World Wide Web

○ Other (please specify)

4. Write a paragraph explaining in more detail why you began to study genealogy elaborating your response in question no. 3

5. Why I continued with genealogy to become a professional genealogist. Select the main reason:

○ I wanted to help others with their work in genealogy

○ I wanted to continue to learn and develop my skills and knowledge in the field

○ The increasing availability of research resources and the Internet made the transition possible

○ The analytical work and puzzles in finding people were so interesting that I wanted to continue to develop my skills as a professional

○ I needed a source of income based on previous education and experience

○ Other (please specify)

6. Write a paragraph elaborating on your response to question number 5: Why you decided to become a professional genealogist.

Professional Genealogy Experience & Education

7. Number of years as a professional genealogist:

◯ less than 1

◯ 2 to 5

◯ 6 to 11

◯ 12 to 19

◯ 20 to 24

◯ 25 to 29

◯ 30 to 35

◯ over 35 years

8. Earned Professional Genealogical Credentials: (Select any that apply.)

☐ Certified Genealogist (CG) year of first certification

☐ Certified Genealogical Lecturer (CGL) year of first certification

☐ Accredited Genealogist (AG) year of accreditation

☐ No credentials

Please indicate the year of certification for the answers selected in Q8:

CG: [＿＿＿＿＿＿]

CGL: [＿＿＿＿＿＿]

AG: [＿＿＿＿＿＿]

9. Honorary Genealogical Credentials: (Select all that apply.)

☐ FASG

☐ FNGS

☐ FUGA

☐ FGBS

☐ FGSP

☐ CG Emeritus

☐ None

☐ Other (please specify)
[＿＿＿＿＿]

Interest in Genealogy and Becoming a Professional Genealogist

10. Highest level of education:

◯ High School

◯ Some College

◯ Bachelor's Degree

◯ Master's Degree

◯ Graduate Studies

◯ PhD

◯ Other doctoral degree

[   ]

Genealogy Educational Certificate:

◯ The Professional Learning Centre, in partnership with the National Institute for Genealogical Studies, University of Toronto

◯ BYU Certificate in Family History

◯ Heritage Genealogical College Certificate in Genealogy/History

◯ Monterey Peninsula Community College Certificate in Family Research Studies: Genealogy

◯ University of Washington at Seattle Certificate in Genealogy and Family History

◯ No Certificate

11. Continuing Education: Which of these institutes, workshops, and seminars have you participated in?
(Select all that apply.)

☐ a. Skill building sessions at NGS and FGS Conferences

☐ b. IGHR Institute for Genealogical and Historical Research (Samford University)

☐ c. NIGR National Institute on Genealogical Research (National Archives)

☐ d. BA Degree courses in Genealogy at Akamai University

☐ e. BA Degree courses in Genealogy at Heritage Genealogy College

☐ f. Monterey Peninsula Community College Family Research Studies: Genealogy courses

☐ g. NGS Home Study Course

☐ h. Boston University Genealogy Research Certificate courses (new program)

☐ i. RIGGS Alliance Workshop

☐ j. None

Interest in Genealogy and Becoming a Professional Genealogist

Please indicate the years you participated in the corresponding continuing education answer choices of "a - i" made in Q11:

a. [   ]

b. [   ]

c. [   ]

d. [   ]

e. [   ]

f. [   ]

g. [   ]

h. [   ]

i. [   ]

12. Professional tasks you carry out as a professional genealogist. (Select all that apply.)

☐ a. Own a bookstore genealogy supply, or publishing business

☐ b. Contract work for clients

☐ c. Write about genealogy

☐ d. Coordinate conferences and events

☐ e. Deliver presentations at seminars and conferences

☐ f. Teach genealogy courses

☐ g. Write books: List number of books written over the last 10 years:

[_____]

If you answered c. "Write about genealogy" from Q12, please select the following:

☐ for pay (commercial publications and services

☐ peer-reviewed research publications

☐ Society and organization publications, without pay

If you answered f. "Teach genealogy courses" from Q12, please select the following:

☐ at local conferences

☐ at national conferences

☐ in continuing education classes

☐ at one or two day scheduled seminars/ workshops

☐ at annual residential classes

☐ in University/college genealogy degree program (s)

☐ in a genealogy certificate program

☐ all of the above

If you answered g. "Write books" from Q12, please select the following:

☐ Commercial publishers

☐ Self-published by client or genealogist

13. Type of work organization in genealogy. (Select all that apply.)

☐ self employed,

☐ employed by a genealogical research or services organization

☐ librarian, curator, archivist

☐ genealogical employment in a non-genealogical organization

☐ teacher in an educational institution

☐ instructor/professor in genealogy higher education

☐ administrator or teacher in a virtual or online environment

☐ Other (please specify)

14. Number of National Conferences attended over the past 5 years:

○ 1 to 2

○ 3 to 5

○ 6 to 10

○ 11 to 15

○ 16 to 20

○ 20 or more

○ None

15. Approximately how much time do you spend in genealogy work per week, including both research and other genealogical related activities?

☐ 5 to 10 hours

☐ 11 to 20 hours

☐ 21 to 35 hours

☐ 36 to 40 hours

☐ 41 to 46 hours

☐ 47 to 55 hours

16. Please write any information that you wish to tell me that you believe I should have asked for in the survey.

Interest in Genealogy and Becoming a Professional Genealogist

Thank you for your cooperation and effort in completing this questionnaire. You will receive a copy of the Summary of the Research Report at the end of the year.

Regards,
LaWanna Lease Blount, Ph.D.